I0458247

Robbie Blackburn

"Hey Dick"

The Story of How I Loved and Lost My Brother

"Hey Dick"
The Story of How I Loved and Lost My Brother

Copyright © 2025 Robbie Blackburn

All rights reserved. No part of this publication may be reproduced, distributed, or transmitted in any form or by any means, including photocopying, recording, or other electronic or mechanical means without proper written permission of the author or publisher, except in the case of brief quotations embodied in critical reviews and certain other noncommercial uses permitted by copyright law.

Paperback ISBN: 978-1-966407-05-8
Hardback ISBN: 978-1-966407-04-1

Published By

The Publishing Pad
www.thepublishingpad.com

Dedication

This book is dedicated to the following people:

To my mom, who has saved my life more times than I can count.

To my dad, who held me up when all I wanted was to fall.

To my wife, Amanda, who has provided unwavering support and unconditional love. You have inspired me in my writing, pushing me to create what I wasn't sure I was capable of creating.

To Dan, who has transcended friendship to become a brother. Thank you for showing up on my lowest day and saving me (and these words).

To Becky, for always putting up with my sarcasm.

And finally, to those who have lost someone special. I dedicate this book to you in hopes that my words and experiences with loss bring you some relief, however fleeting.

"Grief sleeps but doesn't die. At least not until the griever does."
   —**Stephen King,** *You Like It Darker: Stories*

"To have been loved so deeply, even though the person who loved us is gone, will give us some protection forever."
   —**Dumbledore in J.K. Rowling's** *Harry Potter and the Sorcerer's Stone*

"Always."
   —**Severus Snape in J.K. Rowling's** *Harry Potter and the Deathly Hallows*

Table of Contents

Prologue

I killed my brother with a thought.

I know, it sounds ridiculous, and about ten months out of the year, I would agree with you. However, when January and February come around, it is much harder to convince myself of the inanity of such a statement.

You see, I like to write. I've written books, three of them so far, and poems, over eight hundred of those at the time of this writing. One day in roughly the summer of 2007, I thought to myself something along the lines of "I wish I could experience a tragedy so I could have great depth in my pain, and really draw from it and write something profound."

Well, my tragedy happened on February 22, 2008. A train killed my brother as he walked home from a bar on a frigid night. My pain is real, it's never left, and, for multiple reasons, I honestly never expect it to leave.

First, I deserve the pain because I had a thought.

Second, you don't lose your brother—a person you greatly admire and hold up to such a prominent place—in such a manner and hold any expectation of ever getting over it. Evidence shows that before he was hit, he was very confused, perhaps lost, and had fallen multiple times. We suspect he felt nothing, but a suspicion doesn't stop the thoughts that come late in the night when sleep refuses to enter the conversation. These are times when it would be easier to swallow a brick than to actually drift off to the land of nod. In these times, that thought I had in 2007 recurs over and over and repeatedly. To borrow a line from one of my own poems, "it beat beat beat beats in my head on loop and repeat." I killed my brother with a thought. I now always face this as a memory and no longer a thought.

I don't know what I will write here. I will tell some stories about us growing up in rural Ohio together. Some will be firsthand stories, some secondhand stories, some rumors. Probably some will be pieces of multiple memories and even dreams that I have put together over the years. Often I no longer know whether those are memories or dreams, but I consider them to be real because they help keep my brother alive. I will not pretend this will be a great narrative. The memories may be wrong, the timelines out of order. I may jump back and forth in years. I don't know how it's going to look, but I'm going to write it. I aim to write this as a means of helping myself, and if someone like you reads it, I hope I write something that offers you guidance and possibly under- standing, or at the very least lets you know that you are not alone, that we all face these things in our lives. Sometimes we feel like we are alone, but we are never completely alone.

For now, though, this is my adventure, and I'm going to lose myself in some happy memories, sad memories, and probably some mundane ones I didn't think I even recalled. If we are on this journey together, welcome to me. It can get scary in here; I'll freely admit that. We are safe, though. There is always an escape hatch; if things get too hard to deal with, you can close the book and walk away. There are no ties that bind you here. Other than that, let's go.

Life is hard. As Michael Bolton sings in "Jack Sparrow" by The Lonely Island, "This whole town's a pussy," so fuck it.

CHAPTER 1

Storm Clouds

THE SCHOOL YEAR HAS COME TO AN END
I HAVE NOTHING, BUT MAYBE A NEW FRIEND
BUT ONLY ONE OR TWO
HOW MANY MORE DAYS;
ONLY A FEW

LIFE WILL SOON BE A BORE AGAIN
A BASEBALL GAME HERE AND THERE
THAT WE JUST CAN'T WIN.

THE DAYS WILL GROW HOTTER
AS, THANKFULLY, MY LIFE GROWS SHORTER
DAYS OF LONELINESS WILL PLAGUE ME
LIKE A BAD COLD.

TWO MORE YEARS IN THIS HELL
THEN I'LL BE GONE
OUT OF THIS SHITHOLE
NEVER TO BE SEEN AGAIN

MY LIFE WILL BE OVER
NOTHING TO SHOW
EXCEPT A COUPLE OF SO-CALLED FRIENDS
WHO LEFT ME A LONG TIME AGO.

That was the first poem I ever wrote. It started me on the path that led me to writing this book. My biggest fan? My brother. He once took a poem I wrote and sent it in to a company that advertised for poetry submissions and then compiled people's poetry into coffee table books. My poem ended up being published in one of those books; I believe my mom still has a copy somewhere. This just shows how much my brother loved me. It also showed that he thought I possessed talent for writing, and his belief encouraged me to keep writing. I don't think the above poem is great; my skills have improved over the years. That poem was the first, though.

That is a vivid memory, maybe not quite a core memory, but one that sticks out to me clearly. There are others I recall clearly, but most people would call them mundane, almost trivial. I think that once we lose someone, however, there are no such things as mundane or trivial memories of the person who is gone. Every memory becomes a treasure, and we must hold them close and keep them next to our hearts so that they never lose their luster and slip away into the recesses of our minds.

My wife once said to me when we were discussing my brother that since she never met him, she can only know him through my stories and those of others who knew him. She also shared with me a quote she read somewhere: "When you lose a parent, you lose the past. When you lose a child, you lose the future. But when you lose a sibling, you lose both the past and the future." That is so true, if I may wax poetic on this. Beyond true. It also reminds me of a quote from Stephen King's *Wizard and Glass*, which is the fourth book in the *Dark Tower* series, which I am almost certainly going to quote multiple times in this book. The *Dark Tower* series has so many life lessons in it that I quote it almost daily.

A side note before I get to the quote, though: Who introduced me to Stephen King's books? My brother, of course. He was reading a Stephen King book when I was eleven. Wanting to be just like him, the next day at school I checked out *Needful Things* and read it voraciously. That eventually led me to the *Dark Tower* series, which without question changed my life. I don't think I'm being overly dramatic when I say that; at least I hope I'm not. When I get into a dark place in my mind and am struggling to pull myself out of it, I listen to the series again. I have listened to the audiobooks probably fifty times in my life. In Mr. King's coda to *The Dark Tower VI: Song of Susannah*, he quotes his wife as saying, "You're safer when you're with the gunslingers," and that is how I feel. When I listen to the series, I am safer than when I am alone in my mind. I just hope he doesn't sue me for quoting his work so much.

Here is the quote I promised from King's *The Dark Tower IV: Wizard and Glass*:

> So do we pass the ghosts that haunt us later in our lives; they sit undramatically by the roadside like poor beggars, and we see them only from the corners of our eyes, if we see them at all. The idea that they have been waiting there for us rarely if ever crosses our minds. Yet they do wait, and when we have passed, they gather up their bundles of memory and fall in behind, treading in our footsteps and catching up, little by little.

To me, this quote speaks to memories. We live our lives, mundane as they may seem sometimes, and we pass by moments that are insignificant and almost forgotten until a time comes when no more memories are being made. Then we search the deepest recesses of our minds and pull out those mundane, almost innocuous memories just to hold on to the person a little longer.

As I reflect on this right now, one particular memory pops into my head, maybe because storm clouds are gathering in the world around me; this has been a stormy May. I remember sitting in the driveway when I was probably six or seven, so my brother would have been ten or eleven, and we were just playing in a shallow mud puddle that had formed in the turnaround. I vividly remember looking up the road, which would have been to the west, and seeing dark purple clouds rolling toward us. That is it. I don't recall whether we ended up getting a storm or just a cloudy day. Memories like this also come back to me for another reason: I often think about the butterfly effect. Maybe if my brother and I had played in the mud for a minute longer that day, it would have changed the entire course of his life, and he would still be here now. Maybe just one more minute would have led him to a lifetime of different decisions.

CHAPTER 2

The Day of the Accident

I think it is time to get the ugly part out of the way. I don't want this to be a long chapter, so I will not go into gory detail, but it is obviously important to state what happened. When my brother was thirty-two, a train killed him as he was walking home from a bar. He had been drinking. One law firm told me flat out that he had committed suicide, but I just don't see my brother as being the suicidal type. I think he was just walking in a dangerous location because he'd been drinking and his judgement was off.

The day before he died, we were emailing, and he was making plans for the future. He seemed happy. After getting a DUI, serving jail time, and losing an excellent job, he had found another job in Wisconsin. He was in the best place he had been since getting out of jail. My brother was smart—genius-level smart, according to online IQ tests we took—but that doesn't mean addiction would skip him. Alcoholism runs in our family. Our father is a recovering alcoholic. I am very proud to say our dad has been sober for nearly twenty-five years, with a few minor slip-ups here and there.

Back to Bub, though. That is what we called him. At least, our mom's side of the family did. Our dad's side of the family referred to him as Junior because he was named after our dad. Bub was an electrical engineer. His first job out of college was designing lighting systems on submarines in Groton, Connecticut. So, yeah, pretty fucking smart.

Trains almost always trigger me. If I hear a whistle or learn of an accident, I sometimes have a very violent panic attack. A year ago, in East Palestine, Ohio, there was a derailment that was all over social media for a long time afterwards. I had to stay off social media because it was a constant trigger. At a training for my job several years ago, I came close to getting into a fight with two guys who were mocking someone who had been hit by a train and killed that morning. I had to go to the director and tell her. She pulled them aside and told them to stop. It wasn't funny; no jokes like that are funny to me.

I think I'm getting off on a tangent. That won't be the last time it happens. This makes me think about something that crossed my mind while writing my previous books: if I had written them on a different day, the stories could have turned out completely different. I'm sure that is true not just for me but for any artist. If a song, painting, book, or just about anything had been created on a different day, then it could have turned out completely different.

I don't know what else I should say about the accident. I don't really want to say much because it hurts so bad, so I'll just go over how I found out and leave it there. It was a Friday night. I was employed at a children's hospital, where I worked with troubled kids. Fridays were usually rough and wild. I worked on the side with lower-IQ kids, some with special needs, and so on. However, there was a crisis in the other unit that night, so I ran down there to help, and amid my helping, a little girl bit me. Since I'd been bitten, I had to go to the hospital to get checked out. I never got that far. While I was driving to the hospital, my mom called me, and while I may not remember the exact wording, I'm going to try. It went something like this:

Mom: "What are you doing?"

Me: "Going to the hospital. I got bit by a kid."

Mom: "Can you come home?"

Me: "Why? I think they expect me to go back to work."

Mom: "I just need you to come home."

Me: "Why?"

Mom breaks down crying.

Dad gets on the phone. "Get here now; your brother is dead."

I made some sort of inarticulate sound. I still don't know what I said or did when he told me. In my mind I'm sure it was utter denial, but I am not sure what I said, if I said anything. I am pretty sure I screamed.

I don't really remember much after that, except I know I pulled over into the parking lot of an Arby's, which ironically was probably about half a mile as the crow flies from my now-wife Amanda's parents' house. I remember things that happened next, but not the order in which they happened. One thing that happened was that I called my best friend, Dan Striker. We have been friends since literally the first day of kindergarten. I couldn't get a hold of him, so I called his girlfriend at the time, Tiffany, and when she answered, I told her what happened and just screamed, "I NEED DAN!" She promised to get a hold of him and get him to my parents' house to meet me. I also called my then-wife, Audrey, and told her. She said she would come get me or meet me somewhere. I told her I would meet her somewhere between where I was and where we lived. We ended up meeting in a CVS parking lot. I also called my work and, trying to be calm, told them I wouldn't be back and why. The nurse I talked to was very kind and offered to walk out of the job and make sure I was safe. I assured her I would be fine and that my wife was picking me up.

Audrey pulled up in her PT Cruiser, and I just crawled into the back seat and started wailing. She asked me if I knew what had happened, assuming I already knew about the train, which I did not at that point. I don't know if I had been told and forgot or just hadn't been told. I just assumed someone had killed him. That was the only possibility that made sense to me: he'd been mugged and someone murdered him. When she told me, I couldn't believe it. To this day it is still hard to believe. I can't remember anything else we talked about on the ride to my parents' house; I just remember the drive seemed to take forever.

I only remember three other things from that night. The first was getting to my parents' house. There were cars everywhere. I remember falling out of Audrey's car and just screaming over and over, "MOMMY! MOMMY! MOMMY! MOMMY! MOMMY!" I remember going for a walk with my mom that night, and how bitterly cold it was. She gave me what details she knew, and I asked the question myself at that point, even though I didn't think it was possible: "You've talked to him. Did he seem depressed? Do you think it could have been on purpose?" My mom responded with an adamant "NO!"

The third thing I remember is my dad hugging me, crying, and saying repeatedly how worried he'd been because it took Audrey and me so long to get there because it was freezing rain. He said to me, "Not both of them, not both of them the same day."

CHAPTER 3

The Beginning

Jerry Eugene "Bub" Blackburn Jr. was born on July 5, 1975, at Portsmouth Naval Hospital to Jerry Eugene Blackburn and Rosetta Jane (Chase) Blackburn. He weighed 6 pounds 2 ounces, measured 22 inches, had a little bit of blonde hair, and, according to our mother, was the perfect little baby. He had a birthmark on the right side of his right shoulder blade. The honor of cutting the umbilical cord was given to Mom. I asked her just before I started this chapter for some details of Bub's birth, and she gave me this nugget that the nurse said: "God, may you bless this mommy and her son, and by cutting this cord, may their bond never be broken." I can attest that, during my lifetime, that bond was never broken. It most assuredly strengthened.

Even when my brother grew to his full manhood, he struck no one as an imposing figure. He stood five foot four, although he often claimed five foot five, and he weighed no more than 135 pounds at any time I can remember. But he always seemed enormous to me. My little big brother—he was intimidating to me but never mean. He always allowed me to go around with him.

BROTHER

You're my brother,
My family,
My friend and foe
Everywhere you went,
I wanted to go.
I wanted to be just like you
No matter what you wanted to do,

I still can't believe what happened
Since then, it's been a life of confusion
Every day I wake up
Praying for a delusion.
Never before have I wished
To be insane
But I'd do anything
To get that fucking memory
Outta my brain
You're my brother
And I want to make you proud
I miss you more
Than should be allowed.
You're my big brother
And I'm the little
And together we make a pair
We are a tandem
And that
We'll always share
You're my little big brother
And will always be
But what happens
When I hit thirty-three?

I wrote this poem I want to say around 2010. If you count the lines, including the title and the space between the title and the body of the poem, there are thirty-two lines. My brother died at age thirty-two. Without my planning it, the last line became a double entendre. What happens when I hit the thirty-third line, and also, what happens when I hit thirty-three years of age and I become the older brother, at least in terms of years lived? I had it figured out to the day when I would reach the point of having lived longer than him, and it was a very rough day to get through. Perhaps that was a bit obsessive, determining the exact day it would happen. To me it felt important. It's a milestone of life a younger sibling never wants to accomplish. Much like parents never want to outlive their children, no one wants to live longer than a sibling. My brother lived only 15,573 days, and that was not enough, not even close to enough. Years have passed now since I crossed that bitter milestone, and every day I accrue in my life beyond his lifespan leaves a residue behind, a sort of taste that I can't often explain. It is something like sucking on a penny.

Bub was a quiet guy. He would not be the most boisterous person in a room; he would be the guy in the corner, quietly talking to one or two people. I believe he imbibed alcohol to help himself be more social. I think he was very shy around people he didn't know very well, and it was difficult for him to open up. The alcohol took the edge off, made it easier for him to approach people and let them get to know him a little better and quicker. People get through their daily lives however they can. Yet, he had friends, and good friends. He was the type of guy people just enjoyed being around because once you got him to open up, he would be hilarious and could make anyone laugh. He had a quick wit and a dry sense of humor, and he was very fluent in sarcasm.

He loved heavy metal music, Testament and Slayer being his two favorite bands. Also Metallica, probably more pre–Black album, but I remember him liking some songs on that album. He worked his way through college by waiting tables at two different restaurants. After he got his first job in Connecticut, I clearly remember him saying that he couldn't wait to grow his hair long. Which he did—very long, probably down to his mid-back. His brown wavy hair was almost always bunched in a ponytail. He had one tattoo on his shoulder blade depicting Batman wings framing a yellow smiley face wearing a sideways-turned red base-ball cap. He drew it himself in high school, and he always said he would get it as a tattoo someday. That was one of the many goals he set and accomplished. I have a similar tattoo, except instead of the baseball cap, my smiley face has an angel's halo.

My brother frequently discussed three specific goals he set for himself: he would graduate from college, purchase a brand-new Ford Mustang, and run in the New York City Marathon. He accomplished all three goals. Bub had type 1 diabetes; I have type 2. I have often pondered whether God, realizing Bub had achieved all his earthly goals, called him home early to spare him the pain of worsening diabetes and the potential indignity of limb amputation.

CHAPTER 4

Not Just My Brother

"A one-eyed man sees flat. It takes two eyes, set a little apart from each other, to see things as they really are." That is yet another quote from Stephen King's *Dark Tower* series. The main characters in *The Dark Tower V: Wolves of the Calla* come upon a town that needs the help of "the White," the force of good. They are trying to get a good idea of what the town needs from them. One of characters, Jake, a boy of eleven or twelve, wants to stay with his new friend Roland, and he approaches Roland with the idea that seeing the town from multiple perspectives will help them with their evaluation. Roland responds with the above statement, which I think is apt to quote here because seeing my brother from multiple viewpoints, set apart from my own, will give a broader, richer picture of who he was to more people.

Bub was an entire person, not just a flat person of words written on a page. I want to be able to show him in as much depth as possible, give him as much texture as possible, and show that he was not just my brother Bub, but also Jerry to some people who only knew him as that, and Junior to those who knew him as Junior. I want to give him his full due as far as the life he lived. As much as I tried to be around him all the time, he escaped my presence from time to time. He wasn't just my brother, and this isn't just my story; this is his story, at least as much as I can make it about him and not me. I know that this is impossible—I'm the one typing at the keyboard—but if I can introduce you to the brother, I think it is equally important to introduce you to the son, the cousin, the friend, the classmate, and, if I can track any of them down, the coworker. Bub lived a full life in his thirty-two years, one that many people don't get to live, so I want to explore as much about his life as possible.

Also, seeing him through different people's words and memories will bring him to life in a way I had never seen him before. Other people shared memories I would never have known about had I not started this project. Just one person can't write histories; otherwise they will come across not so much as history as perhaps a biography. So, as opposed to sharing just my stories and memories, I will sprinkle amongst them the stories and memories of various other people who were connected to my brother. In doing so, I aim to create a multidimensional picture of him and allow us all to enjoy more of his life.

It is impossible to know someone else's entire life. I think sometimes it isn't even possible for us to know our own entire lives. This is not just because we forget things—or block them out, in cases of deep trauma—but because we evolve over time. We change, in all ways, physically, mentally, emotionally, and in some cases spiritually. As those changes occur, we can change fundamentally. With that being said, I want to put my brother in the middle of a circle and fill in as many of the spaces around him as possible to ensure that we all get to see a fuller picture of the baby, the boy, the adolescent, and the adult that he grew into. Doing this feels important; it feels right as the best way to honor his legacy.

CHAPTER 5

Anger

I think about this project a lot, about how I want to arrange it. I want to paint a picture of my brother with words—not just a picture but a living memory, a document that lives on forever, one that may continue to grow as time passes. Should I just list memories and tell stories about his life? I would like to do that, but a major part of this project is about my coming to grips with his death as well, so I think I will waver back and forth between his life and his death and how each affected me, my family, and everything else. He impacted us before he died; I want to show how that happened. Life wasn't always about recovering from losing him. There were good and bad times, before and after he was lost to us.

While there were good times, I must start with the bad, because it is the bad that has me sitting here writing this memoir. So the first thing I want to talk about is anger. When I say anger, I am talking vitriolic levels of righteous anger. *Righteous* is the right word to use here, because I often direct the anger at God, whatever it is I call God. I still don't have a clear definition of what that would be. At certain points of my life, I would have said I was an atheist; at others, an agnostic. However, now I'd say that I believe in something, but I'll never believe in a religion. I think the two are different.

If anyone has ever seen the movie *Legends of the Fall* with Brad Pitt, he's the misfit brother Tristan, the wild child, the recluse, a guy who can't be tamed because of the wildness still within him. He attempts to kill a bear in the beginning. There's also a scene where he and his two brothers go to Canada to join the military so they can fight "the Huns" in Germany. When they are there, Tristan's youngest brother gets caught in mustard gas and barbed wire and then is machine-gunned to death by German soldiers. Tristan tries to save him but is too late.

He gets his brother out of the barbed wire and then cuts his heart out to send it back home. As he is doing this, he is crying and screaming, "GOD DAMN YOU, GOD!" I feel this scene to the very core of my being and soul. It radiates through my bones. It's a hard thing to watch, but I understand because I feel that anger toward God for taking my brother away from me.

With that boldly stated, I also want to mention that at the funeral of my ex-wife's grandma, I was talking to the officiating clergy. I was telling him about how angry I was with God. I said that I felt somewhat guilty because we weren't supposed to be angry with God.

His response was, "Why not? God allows us free will. You're allowed to be angry. You lost your brother in a very unfortunate accident. Anger is going to be a natural part of that."

I then asked, "But if I'm angry with God, won't he be angry at me in return because I questioned his plan?"

He said, "Not at all. He understands your anger because he can't tell you his plan."

"So, while I'm so angry, it's okay to direct it at God?"

"Absolutely."

This conversation became part of a poem I titled *Waking Nightmare*.

> I still blame
> God
> And why not
> I was told
> He has the shoulder
> To hold
> This boulder
> While I
> Sit and smolder

I'll include the entire poem at the end of this book. That conversation helped me a lot. I expected no one, especially not a member of the clergy, to tell me it is okay to be angry with God.

The anger I have felt and continue to feel is not only directed towards an entity I choose to call God. I spread so much anger around that it becomes almost invisible and therefore seemingly insignificant. I get angry at myself, my parents, society, the conductor, the bartender, the other patrons. I get angry at the friends who perpetuated my brother's drinking, at our ancestors who allowed the addiction gene to thrive and continue. Most of all, I get angry at him—my brother. I want to scream and rage at him for being so stupid about the entire situation. Then, however, I remember alcoholism is a disease, and without proper treatment—hell, even acknowledgement—it will continue on and on.

My brother was so smart. How could he have allowed himself to get so deep into trouble with alcohol? He had gotten multiple DUIs. Shouldn't that have been a lesson learned? Then I think: He was walking, not driving, so he learned that much at least. Then the anger will rise again, and I feel that, ultimately, he was sentenced to death for a DUI. It was a DUI in Connecticut that led him to be in Wisconsin on February 22, 2008. Some days it's hard to hold onto the anger at him. Other days, it's almost as easy as breathing. When I have one of those days, I continuously remind myself that he didn't do this on purpose. He would never have put our mom through this intentionally, let alone me. I feel strongly about that, regardless of what some asshole lawyers told me. Not that it would have tarnished my memory of my brother if it had been suicide. Suicide is not a sign of weakness or anything else negative. It is just an end for some people, me included. I've thought about it often, attempted it several times.

To be clear, there is no part of me that thinks my brother's death might have been intentional. Suicide isn't what happened; it's not why I'm angry. It was just a terrible, shitty accident. The only reason I get angry at the lawyer who tried to tell me it was suicide is because of his complete lack of empathy. He made it seem like my brother was less than a person and was stupid to have landed himself in a situation that ultimately took his life.

* * *

This is an email my brother sent to me after my physician bluntly confronted me about not taking care of myself and addressing my diabetes:

diabetes

As we talked, you need to take care of yourdelf. I know its hard, (trust me l do) but you have to try.

You have at least two people that love you more than the world itself, and anything that would happen to you would be be just too devastating. and i can't live with that. Because I am a role model to you and because of that I try to be the best that I can be, and that is the biggest reason I am where I am today. Don't worry about money, what your insurance won't cover I will, but I plan on being around a long time, and those plans include you.

your brother

This email may appear in other parts of this book because depending on my mood it means different things to me at different times. Here, I'm referencing my anger that he isn't still here, telling me to take care of myself. He could have been around to help me as I get better with managing the diabetes. Then I recall he sent this to me a mere two years before he died—a death that could have been prevented if he had just taken care of himself. Yet he didn't. Then sometimes there's anger toward myself when I read it because he said, bluntly, that he would be there for me, yet when the tables were turned, I didn't have the courage to confront him. I feel like a coward because maybe he was waiting for someone to confront him about his drinking, and I failed him. I am the one with the psychology degree. Why couldn't I have seen signs of cries for help if they were there? How many did I miss? How many did I ignore because I was busy getting engaged and planning a wedding and being a newlywed, caught up in my life and selfish? I've kept this email for a long time because it means so much to me. It did at the time, for sure, because I felt his love and support, which I still feel, yet now I feel disappointed that the long time he planned on being around was only about two and a half years more.

CHAPTER 6

The Plague of Dreams

I think about what Glen Bateman says in Stephen King's *The Stand* when he first meets Stu and they are talking: "The only bane of my life has been my dreams. Ever since boyhood I've been plagued by amazingly vivid dreams."

Since the accident, I too have been plagued by vivid dreams. Some of them are terrible, some of them are amazing. Some are disturbing and leave me feeling a sense of despair for the entire day. One in particular gave me the will to go on after my first wife left me. I wrote about it here:

EXHAUSTION

I grew tired of explaining
Why my will to live was draining
My death has been decades in waiting
A life lived ill-fated
A frame of mind, there was no escaping
Willing to give that which can only be taken
I'm nothing if not forsaken
A tree that bears fruit that does not need shaking
I didn't know how long it had taken
But I feel as though I have been awakened

I wondered if I could feel again
And if I could, when
I sat back and pondered this to no end
I'm not likely to have anyone but another friend
A natural-born loser who doesn't know how to win

"HEY DICK"

A small victory is all I could afford now and then
But a victory is too much to say it in

What could I do that I never did
I cried I lied I hid
I threw a fit
I said fuck it
I wanted to quit
I vowed to take no shit
But here I am standing with a mouth full of it

What was I except maybe a means to an end
Just someone to fuck with and say we can't even be friends
I'm no Andy Dufresne
I can't crawl through a river of shit
And come out the other side clean
I'm stuck in the middle covered in it

I know what it's like to be thrown away
I know the feeling of going to bed alone
At the end of the day
I know what it's like to be so angry
You can't find the words to say
I've broken glass and punched a wall
I have sat and watched your shit burn
I asked god why the fuck it couldn't be my turn

I died. I really did. This spring.
I stopped breathing
I took so many pills my breath stopped
I could feel my body pulling me back
I did everything I could every ounce of me fought
I didn't want to come back
Me being dead would be your fault

I wanted you to feel one last thing
Something that would never go away
I wanted you to be overcome with guilt
That would have been enough for me

I know it wouldn't be grief
No chance of that because you don't care
As I fought for my death
I looked inside myself and thought
You wouldn't even feel guilt
You'd just brush my death off
As easy as you threw me away
You'd just go ho-hum and go about your day

You are an apathetic being
Nothing is felt except for what you hold
Selfishness
That's all you are. Selfish.
I fucking hate you.
I never thought I could say that, but it's true
I fucking hate you. I said it again.
I don't care what happens to you.
Because I fucking hate you.

You destroyed me
Worst of all, you lied to me
Right to my face,
With absolute calculation
And menace
You claim it was to protect me
But I did everything I could to tell you
All I wanted was the truth
But that wasn't in you
Until you were assured an escape plan

"HEY DICK"

A piece of shit half a man
Fuck him too
And fuck you three
Because one fuck you to you
Wouldn't ever be enough

Remember years ago I told you
That I would always die for you
Well, I died for you.
My breath stopped
It wasn't just in my chest caught
I was done, my last breath taken
There was no light, no open arms
Just eternal darkness
Something I thought would be alright
If I couldn't spend my life with you
I will say it again.
I died. I inhaled my last breath
I was moments, perhaps seconds from death

I fought for my death
Because I hated my life.
Most of all, I hated myself
I felt I was beyond help
No cure in a bottle, no cure in talk
It was for my death I fought
And I had it almost won
I was slipping away
Then I saw my brother's face
And heard the words he had to say

"Hey dick, this isn't you
You've changed and not for the good
Knock this shit off

I don't want to see you yet"
And then just like that
I no longer sought
The death for which I fought
I wanted to live
I wanted to see another day
Up out of bed, I shot
Out went what was my last breath or so I thought
In and out breaths I drew
And thanked my brother for the talk
And said, "fucking Bub I still so love you."

Without a doubt, that poem is about a lot more than just my dream about my brother coming to me and saying his traditional greeting of "Hey dick," but I thought it was important to include the entire piece in this book because of the nature of what I was going through. When I wrote it, over five years ago now, I didn't think I could ever share it with anyone. I was ashamed to admit I was in such a dark place, so I kept it to myself for quite a while. When I did share it, however, people told me how good and emotionally compelling it is. It's long, and it was hard to write from an emotional standpoint, but, as with almost everything I write, it was done in a matter of minutes. I write quickly most of the time; once I have an idea, it just flows out of me. I don't know if I'd call it a true stream of consciousness or not, but it sure is something—especially if, when I'm done and I read it again, I think for a change that something I wrote is actually pretty good.

Dreams have always been intense for me. As a younger person—say, between the ages of nine and thirteen—I would go to bed and mentally flip through topics like they were in the *TV Guide*, choosing what I was going to dream about that night. Most nights, I could do it and do it well. I can also lucidly dream, which can be very cathartic because when I know I'm dreaming, I can say and do things I wouldn't or couldn't do in the waking world—things like telling off my dad when he hurt me; punching the former president of this country because he sucks; or being more assertive with the opposite sex, something I struggled with because of shyness in my teens and early adulthood.

This ability to dream vividly comes with a curse, though. Sometimes my dreams leave me in a dark, despairingly dull and ominous place for an entire day or more. For example, my mom and I never fight. I don't recall one argument in my entire life. However, once I dreamt we got into an argument, and the entire day I felt like she was mad at me. The dream was so vivid and the emotions so real that I mistook them for memories. Finally, I mustered the courage to call her, and she was happy to hear from me; the events in the dream had never happened.

How do I lay out for you the dreams I've had since the accident—both the terrible ones and the amazing ones? When I blow breath through the keyhole of memory and the tumblers turn, revealing the path before us, what signpost will we encounter first? Do we climb the mountain carrying my burden, where it holds us back and slows us down? Or do we start at the top and come down, where my burden may push us to the bottom more quickly, ending the worst part sooner but risking a fall? I will be hurt either way, so the question is: do I want to heal sooner or delay the worst of the hurt until later? Either way, the hurt will come, and the tears will flow, as they always do. Unfortunately, the burden doesn't lighten with the passage of time. There is no lightening the load, so to speak, as each story is told. These are not to be cast off to the side of the path. They are forever and always firmly attached and borne on my shoulders.

THE PLAGUE

When dreams become plague
That filter out the day
All the fears that you've come to know
Make their appearance
When the eyes go closed
The darkness has become

A master of pretend
Leads me down the path
Telling I can go home again
I wish to not go
Back to where I've been

The truth in these lines resonates deeply with me. Dreams sometimes blur the lines between reality and darkness, causing me to lose touch with the waking world. Some dreams are so terrible that I can hardly find the words to describe them.

Drawing from the *Dark Tower* series once again (*The Dark Tower IV: Wizard and Glass*), dreams are "mud pies of the mind," and boy, do they dirty up the works of trying to get through life sometimes. These nightmarish visions often leave me drained, struggling to shake off the residual fear and despair they cast over my day. They cause me to forget the waking world, and they want to hide in the darkness, making it difficult to navigate my reality.

Oh, the burden of some of these dreams I have had; I can't set them aside for wanting. They must be carried forever. Some days they weigh more heavily on me, while other days I adjust to their dragging me down, but their presence is forever.

I have two recurring dreams that have haunted me almost since the time of the accident. Forgive me if I go into too much detail, for I do not really want to do so. Part of me hopes that in doing so, I might cleanse them from my mind.

The first one—I think I had it within the first month after he died—is the most frequent dream I have had about it. I don't know if I have ever told anyone the amount of detail I am going to here. I think it is unlikely that I ever have because they hurt too much, so here goes anyway.

I am standing along the tracks, and I know something is wrong because I am looking and yelling for my brother, but he is nowhere to be found. I almost always start near the railroad tracks where we grew up in Hammondsville, Ohio. There is a little convenience store there, has been for years. I come out of the store and see the tracks. I sense something is wrong and I need to find him. He isn't with me in the store, but I sense he should be.

I immediately run over to the tracks and yell his name, running up and down the tracks, but I see nothing. Then I see something that looks like a bag of trash. I run to it anyway and pick it up; it is trash. I dump it out on the ground, and there is nothing I recognize inside it. Suddenly, off in the distance, I hear a train whistle and the pounding of the engine and wheels on the track. I bend down and touch the track and know the train is coming fast. Inside, I know my brother is in trouble. I scream his name, and in my mind, I hear him yelling for me, "Robb, help me!"

As soon as he finishes this call for help, I am instantly transported to near where he is, lying between the tracks. I can see from fifty feet away that his head and mouth are bleeding. He is fully conscious but unable to move. I tell him to get up, but he says he can't. Everything is too heavy. I scream at him to get up as I see the approaching headlight coming around the bend. I cry and scream at him. I'm still thirty or forty feet away.

I run as fast as I can. I can feel the frigid February air around me. I'm crying; the tears instantly freeze to my face. I feel the pain of those tears like acid on my skin. The footing is treacherous—rocks, cast-off trash, logs, and ice are obstacles I must navigate. I don't do very well; I trip at least twice, sometimes more. Finally, I arrive at where he is lying, and I'm screaming at him to get up. "GET UP, GOD DAMMIT! WHAT THE FUCK ARE YOU DOING?"

He responds, "I can't move. Help me."

I bend down to pick him up, sliding my arms under him, but my hands and arms pass right through him. I can feel the cold ground beneath him but can't feel any weight from him. I try to lift, thinking it is just all part of the adrenaline rush. I will just lift him, and he will be safe. The train whistle is louder; the sound of it approaching is deafening. He is screaming, but I can't hear what he's saying. The train is now feet away, and I know what is about to happen. I try to put myself with him, try one more time to lift him, and make the decision that we will go together. I feel the impact of tons of steel hitting me, and I'm thrown back. I almost always awaken screaming.

Upon awakening, I can feel the impact on my body. I hurt everywhere. I feel a sensation as if blood running down my head. The spit has dried in my mouth. The screams tear from me, whether they have voice or just air; they don't always have both. The screams hurt. I feel like I'm ripping my throat out from the inside. I know it makes little sense. That is just the feeling I have when I am awake. I have an intense feeling of dread, hopelessness, and guilt. He asked for my help; he begged for my help. My brother, who really never asked me for anything, was begging me for help, and I failed him.

The second recurring dream has a very similar setting and start. Sometimes I recognize the dream, but still I must partake in the events as if they are set in stone. Perhaps they are. Perhaps this is my punishment for being a worthless human being, for killing my brother with a thought. The key difference between this dream and the other one I have is that I arrive differently at the scene. In this dream, I am usually running up the tracks from the crossing where he ended up being found. I am sprinting up the tracks as the train approaches from the opposite side of him. I'm screaming "He's not trash! He's not fucking trash!" This I know is from the accident report and the interview with the conductor, or whatever he is called. He said he thought my brother was a bag of trash on the tracks. So much about that report hurts, but that part may hurt the most. At the end of his life, my brother was mistaken for a bag of trash.

He screams at me as I approach, "Robb, help me!"

Once again, I feel the frigid February air as it freezes my tears to my face. My breath is freezing going in and hot coming out. The stitch in my side is debilitating. I try to scream at him to move, but the deafening sounds of the approaching train, the engine, the whistle, the pounding of my heart in my ears make it impossible for me to hear myself; I don't know if I make any sounds. Skidding to a stop beside him, I go to the ground, then I try to scoop him up. My arms pass right through him. I am the ghost in this dream. I try again, and again and again and again and again, beginning to scream. The screams are ripping my throat to pieces; trying over and over and nothing is working, screaming more and more, the rips in my throat feel as though they are bleeding, the coppery taste fills my mouth, the tears streak down my face and freeze, leaving acidic streaks, as it were, the pain in my heart as it breaks knowing I am to be of no help, I am screaming, cussing at the world. I step back and watch as my brother's life is taken from him. I scream again because the world—my world, I feel like, at the very least—just ended, and I was too cowardly to go with him. Because my punishment will be to live.

With this dream, too, I almost always wake up screaming and usually crying. I feel helpless, hopeless; I feel a dread so heavy it is almost palpable. My heart is pounding, I am sweating, and I'm breathing as if I have just run through a frigid February night. The coldness of the night lingers; the guilt of it all crushes my soul. If I am going to have these dreams, I prefer the first one, because in that one, I get to die too.

After either of these dreams, life is not very fun to live. I feel shaky, jittery, on edge, and irritable. My brother is always heavily on my heart, but on the occasions that I have these dreams, it's not a pleasant feeling. His memories give me no joy, no happiness. Nothing but pain. I know he would hate to know I am saying this, because I doubt he would ever want to cause me pain.

I've had many other dreams about him over the years. They vary in their content, but they always seem to have one primary theme: that he stays at my parents' house for the holidays and never leaves. He will be there for months. I ask him all the time in the dreams about his job and paying his bills, but he always shrugs me off. In a lot of these dreams, I know he is dead but he does not, and neither do my parents. I am the only one who is aware that he is dead. I feel like if I tell people that he is, I will be punished. Many times, when I have these dreams, he won't speak to me nor even look at me. I always awaken from these dreams with a sense that he is angry with me because I killed him, and he knows I killed him. I killed him with a thought, and because he is now in heaven, he knows everything I've ever thought, and he hates me. A lot of the guilt I feel around the anniversary of his death is centered on this notion that he is angry at me for killing him. That is why he interacts with my parents but never with me.

I have always found it difficult to talk to people about these dreams. I haven't talked to a therapist about them, mostly because I feel like I'm being stupid. I also just have a hard time dealing with these dreams when I'm awake. The effects linger. I see flashes of the dreams in my daily life for days after I have them. I feel random twinges of the pains I felt in the nightmares. The depression is a heavy burden, more so than it normally is. I feel drained physically, mentally, emotionally, and spiritually. Also, I am afraid to go back to sleep. I don't want to have the dreams again. I can't have them if I am awake. Sometimes I write poems to help me.

Here is one I wrote February 19, 2012, after awakening from one of these dreams:

OMNIBENEVOLENT NO MORE

Around four years ago today
My life changed
In an unthinkable way
God or whatever
Took my brother's precious life away
So many people say
It'll get better
But it hasn't yet
I haven't had a single ounce
Of anger disperse
Days number 1-4-6-2
And it still hurts
Getting no better
But probably worse
I wanna go outside

"HEY DICK"

And scream and curse
Beat my chest
And let my vocal cords burst
No amount of physical pain
Can compete
with the pain
Of every heartbeat.
A thousand memories
Flooding my brain
All vying for the main screen
Which is dominated
Not by memory but a dream
Where I'm looking on
Unable to move
Unable to scream
I wake without relief
Just more anger buried deep
I've heard time and again
That this is god testing me
So if that's the case
Then I failed miserably
My faith has weakened
Not been renewed
God is no longer
What I viewed
All good and powerful
That idea is skewed
I think you don't care
All that much
We've fucked up over and over
So, you've washed your hands of us
So, we are here
Wallowing in what's left behind
You don't care if when

We are in trouble we look to the sky.
I know this is blasphemous
But I don't care
I am full of anger
And I need to direct it somewhere
Life has been fucked up
That ain't fair
So much wrong
So little right
Only escape
Is to sleep at night
But I suffer dreams
Of the past
Everything straining
Threatening the clasp
Sometimes I feel
I'm cracking like glass.

There are other ways my dreams have affected my grieving, sometimes hindered it, set it back, even. My ability to dream lucidly has made grieving more difficult. This was true especially at the beginning of the process. I would have these dreams where I knew my brother was both dead and alive, or at least I felt like he was both dead and alive. Upon waking from these dreams, I sometimes fell asleep again and intentionally had one or two more dreams where he was still alive to me. I did this mostly because it was just a chance to experience him, touch him, talk to him, and love him. My heart and mind longed to linger in the dream version of reality. If only I could have passed the rest of this lifetime in those brief moments upon waking, spending all the breaths I have left whispering my brother's name onto the wind. A time, however brief, could be held for an eternity, and he would still be alive. Alas, the moment would fade, reality would weigh upon me, and the depth of the sadness would impress itself on me as the knowledge reestablished itself that he is indeed gone from this life. Reality was always hard for a while after these moments. I doubt that this differs greatly from the experience of most victims of unspeakable tragedies. I think that, for me, the intensity of the feeling was stronger because of my capacity for lucid dreaming.

For weeks in the immediate aftermath of his death, I had a complete feeling of unreality. I kept thinking I was still dreaming. I felt like I was sleepwalking through the days and nights. Dreaming was more reality to me than anything else. I would intentionally smack myself against things like tables, walls, and doors to feel something and try to wake myself up. It never worked. Slowly but surely, reality seeped into that dreamlike state. However, to this day, sixteen and a half years later, remembering that he is gone still hits me with a feeling of unreality. I can't feel myself for a minute or two. I start to waver, as if there is a disturbance between the layers of the dreaming and waking worlds, and I slip into another life where my brother is still alive. Then suddenly I am back, and the pain hits again. It feels fresh, and the thoughts and memories flood back into my mind. They drown in me in their reality and intensity. They wound me, as once the news did when it was new. Tears well in my eyes, my heartbeat speeds up, and my throat feels as though it is closing, like I'm suffering from anaphylaxis.

CHAPTER 7

The Early Days

W orking on this project for the last couple of weeks has cost me sound and quality sleep. I have had more nightmares than usual. Perhaps this is the fair medium of exchange for going down the path of memory. I think of a line from the R.E.M. song "Leave": "Where is the road I follow, to leave, leave?" I sometimes think that it is hard to go down that road, but then it is just as hard, if not harder, to stray off that path and back to the world. Maybe that is what I owe my brother. I have always felt that the amount of pain you feel for a loss is in direct correlation to the amount of love you have for what has been lost.

I often go back and watch the video of Billy Bob Thornton talking about losing his brother. He said, "I have to really force myself to think that things are going to be okay in terms of worrying about my family, or myself or one of my friends [. . .]. There's a melancholy in me that never goes away. I'm fifty percent happy and fifty percent sad at any given moment. [. . .] I don't want to forget my brother, and I don't want to forget what it felt like when he died, because he deserves it; that's how important he was to me. So, if I have to suffer and if I have to be sad for the rest of my life, and if I have to be lonely without him [. . .], then that's the way I honor him."

The sadness I feel never really goes away, as Billy Bob states. At any time, I can fall into the pit of sadness because even to this day, some sixteen years after his death, the fact that he is gone surprises me sometimes.

I have enjoyed some memories, though. They are good, even though they hurt. They make me happy and sad.

There's a story I want to tell from before I had any actual memory, because I was a baby unable to even walk yet. My mom has told this story to me a few times, and I always enjoy hearing it because I think it says something about what kind of person my brother was. Early one morning, Bub, being the sweetest little five-year-old boy ever and wanting to thank our mom for being the best mom ever, decided to make her breakfast. He got the milk and cornflakes out and poured her a bowl of cereal with no problems. However, he knew our mom didn't start the day without a cup of coffee. Dad had already gone to work, and Mom was still asleep. It was to be a big surprise. He believed he was big enough to make coffee because he had seen her do it many times. He put the pot of water on the stove and set it to boil. He put the coffee and creamer into the cup. When the water boiled, he grabbed a dish towel because the pot was too hot. The dish towel fell into the flame of the propane gas stove and immediately caught fire. Bub panicked and dropped the towel. The resulting flames melted the plastic cabinet door beside the stove. However, even in his five-year-old panicked mind, Bub still had the presence to think of his baby brother in his room. He took care of me, then woke up our mom.

Mom smelled the smoke and melted plastic and rushed to the kitchen to put out the fire, averting disaster. Bub, crying so hard he could barely speak, sputtered out, "I just wanted to make you breakfast."

Mom said, "Oh, thank you so very much!" while giving him a big hug. After a few moments, she asked, "Where's the baby?" Bub responded with, "He's safe." Then he led her to the closet of my room, where he had taken me out of my bed and placed me underneath a bunch of blankets. I was red-faced and sweating but otherwise unharmed. My mom cried with relief, picked me up, and hugged us both.

My mom always ends the story the same way: "That was the best cup of coffee I ever had, and I ate those cornflakes even though I hate them, but that day they tasted so good. I can still see his little face. He was so scared."

This is one of those stories that have become memories, and it shows my brother's character from a very early age. He was a selfless person who wanted to do good for others. Even when things went wrong in the kitchen that day, his first instinct wasn't to save himself but to save me. I've encountered many people in my life, but I don't know many whose first instinct, especially at age five, would have been to prioritize someone else's safety over their own.

A ROSE BLOOMS

A rose blooms
In a time
When frosty morn looms
When the sign
Is seasons change
In spring the flower
Is time to grow
When hope springs eternal
And the grass will soon
Need a mow
Even in summer
During hottest days
The flower is expected
To stay
But not the fall
That's the end of all
No red or blue or white or pink
A birthday present from above
So just when I think
The tears were over
A rose blooms
In October.

There is no graveyard to visit for my brother's final resting place. He was cremated. Most of his ashes reside in my parents' home. For a time, when we were not sure what to do with them, I drove around with them in my car. I had a bottle of Mountain Dew sitting beside him, since he could now drink it, diabetes no longer being an issue for him. Then my parents built a concrete slab memorial for him in their backyard. I couldn't stand to not have him with me once I gave him back to my parents, so my mom came up with a solution. She found a small ceramic container with a black cat on it, reminiscent of Bub's all-time favorite cat, AJ, and then my dad—and I have absolutely no idea how he could have done this—opened up the urn, took a few of the ashes out, and placed them in that vessel. In every vehicle I've owned since then, Bub has hung from my rearview mirror. He travels with me as my companion and my protector. My protector, always.

The poem above reflects that protection. At a low point in my life, I had told no one how depressed I was, but I was down and feeling hopeless and helpless. It was a couple of years after my brother died. I felt stuck in my job; I could make extra money, but that meant I had to be there more. I had to be there more because of personal poor decisions and a wife who had a spending habit she couldn't get under control. At that job, you see, I worked what is called a block shift. I stayed at work for three nights at a time. When I worked overtime, I stayed even longer. On my days off, I worked a second job in the psychiatric unit at a hospital; that job was part time. I was in a rut and had resigned myself to a life of complete and utter exhaustion. I saw nothing beautiful anymore.

Then in October, on my birthday, my mom went out to my brother's memorial and saw that a single rose had bloomed on the rosebush she had planted there. I took that as a sign that my brother was letting me know that even though that the season I was currently going through in my life wasn't what I expected, beauty could and would eventually arise from those times.

Even in the afterlife, he is looking after me. Protecting me. He is as willing to cover me in a shroud of love now as he was a baby in the closet with blankets. A big brother's job is to protect, always. Just because he has gone on to the next realm, the job doesn't end.

My mom picked that rose and put it in a mason jar. I still have it. I keep it in my freezer. I never take it out, but once in a while I look at it and remember that always, always there can be beauty in the most unexpected of times. Hope springs eternal in the heart that carries love within its walls.

My brother, the protector, wasn't always ready to take on that role, however. My mom recently told my wife and me a story about the first time he met me. I was born early—two and a half months early, to be exact. I was in an incubator and separated from everyone, and only my mom could visit me. My brother was staying with my Uncle Jack while my mom was in the hospital giving birth to me, a process that took thirty-six hours. I was in a hurry, then not so much, apparently.

Bub had wanted a sister. He repeatedly told my mom to get him a sister. When he first saw me, I had, as I still often do, kicked my leg up in my sleep and crossed it over my other one, rolling to the side. He said to my mom, "Her butt is showing!"

My mom replied, "That's your brother, not a sister."

Bub was not happy. He insisted I was a girl because during my mom's pregnancy, all the old wives' tales pointed to me being a girl. Everyone told my brother he was getting a little sister. He was much more excited about having a sister than a brother. My mom then went into the isolation room, picked me up, and carried me to the window to show my brother that I was, in fact, a little brother, not a sister.

His disappointment continued. As relayed to me over the years by him and others, he told people the only reason he got a little brother and not the sister he wanted was "because he was on sale during the Blue Light Special at Kmart." He frequently begged my parents to return me and get him his sister.

I apparently grew on him, though. Not long after my birth, we moved to Louisiana for a year. My brother attended kindergarten there. The other kids, my mom said, picked on him all the time, and it made him very sad. When he would come home from school, he would go into my room, where I was in my crib, and tell me all about how the kids were being mean to him. He would then play with me or just touch my hands. These moments planted the seeds that put down the roots and eventually bore the fruits of a strong bond of brotherhood.

I have one memory of being in Louisiana, even though I wasn't over eighteen months old when we left. It is of him and me sitting on the back porch steps. Maybe it's not a memory; maybe it's a memory forged by a photograph taken. I feel strongly that it is an actual memory, reinforced by the photograph below. I had a painting made of it as a Christmas present for my mom, and she has the painting on her wall. My dad carries us around in his pocket: I had the same image engraved on a leather wallet, along with pictures of his two favorite dogs and one of my mom.

Bub and I behind our home in Louisiana.

CHAPTER 8

Road Trips

Anyone who reads, or, as I do more often these days, listens to books will understand this. There is a particular character in one of my favorite books who, when I listen, I picture as an eleven-year-old Bub. That book is Stephen King's *IT*, and the character is Big Bill, as the kids in the "Losers Club" call him.

The scene that drives that point home is when Eddie is driving north from Boston. "Bill knew stuff to do. Places to go. Things to see. Bill was never up against it. When you ran with Bill you ran to beat the devil and you laughed."

That is how I always felt with Bub. No matter what, he was up for an adventure; most often, it was his plan, and he executed it. He did not seem to live his life in fear of anything. I can't really remember my brother ever being scared—not even when Atlanta Braves fans threatened to kick our asses when we were leaving a Pirates game one night. This was under part of the old Three Rivers Stadium, where the Pirates played their home games. Some Braves fans were standing outside the visitor's locker room holding a sign for the TV station TBS that said, "TBS: The Best in Sports." The implication was that TBS didn't just stand for Turner Broadcasting System, it also stood for The Best in Sports. Chipper Jones, who was signing autographs, repeated aloud what the sign said.

Well, my best friend, Dan, had a better idea. He screamed at the Braves fans, and at Chipper: "TBS: The Braves Suck!"

The Braves fans, who were drunk, made a move toward us like they wanted to fight. Bub was probably eighteen, maybe nineteen; Dan and I would have been fourteen or fifteen, I'm guessing. When they came at us, I ran. I am a lover, not a fighter. Dan and my brother just stood there like, "Bring it on, fuckers." I was scared for sure, but I can look back and laugh at that now. Even immediately afterward, it was funny.

I have taken several road trips in relation to Bub over the years. Some were with him, some were for him, and some were just to drive and think about him and let myself miss him in a safe space, where I could cry my tears to a steering wheel and let the highway miles drift behind me as I work my way down the road to where we will meet again.

One road trip I took by myself happened in July 2019. I was newly divorced, had no ties to anything, and wanted to go somewhere. So, I went to Boston. Bub and I had gone there together in June 2005 for a baseball game at Fenway Park. It was on Father's Day, which was fitting because he was like a second father to me. The Red Sox were playing our hometown favorites, the Pittsburgh Pirates. That day, we wanted to do all the touristy things people do when they go to Boston: Fenway, the Freedom Trail, and, probably the most touristy thing of all, eat at the Cheers bar. The only goal of those three that we accomplished fully was the game at Fenway. The Freedom Trail was longer than we expected, much like the wait for a table at Cheers.

Back to 2019: I rented a vehicle for the drive to Boston. I stopped on the way and visited a friend for a couple of days, then got a hotel room just outside Boston. The first day I was there, I walked the entire Freedom Trail. It was long; I can't remember how many miles it was. I hurt afterward, but it was worth it because the starting point (where I also ended) is in Boston Common, and next to Boston Common is the Public Garden, and right across from that is the Cheers bar. So, I went in, waited for an hour, and got myself a beer, just like Norm and the guys. I carried my brother in my pocket that entire day. Below is the picture I posted on Facebook.

It took fourteen years for us to accomplish what we set out to do in 2005. We did it, though, and, like so many other things, we did it together.

Bub has finished the freedom trail and eaten at Cheers today. I feel accomplished.

My Facebook post after my trip to Boston. I brought Bub with me.

One other point about this trip: When I went into Boston, I parked in a parking garage near the harbor and then walked to Boston Common to start the Freedom Trail. After walking the trail and then eating at Cheers, I was too tired to walk back to the parking garage. So I took a subway train. That was a mistake. I panicked when I was in the waiting area for the train, got on the wrong one, went the wrong direction, and had an almost full-scale meltdown in the middle of the car, where I was standing. I started to hyperventilate and cry. An older lady who had a seat asked me if I was okay. I said, "No. I'm freaking out."

She told me to take her seat, and once the train stopped, she walked with me onto the platform and to the stairs. She talked to me for a few minutes, making sure that I was okay. She said she didn't want to leave me, that she understood panic attacks. She didn't ask why or anything, she just talked to me in a calm voice for a brief period. I don't know what she said, but it helped, and when I calmed down and told her that I was going to be fine, I did not know where I was. I ended up getting on the Lyft app and ordering a ride back to my car. I guess it was just an emotional day, and my defenses weren't strong enough to hold up against that trigger. A positive came out of the Lyft ride, however. I talked to the driver and learned that people could make decent money driving for rideshare services. When I returned home from my trip, I tried it. Driving for Uber and Lyft for the next couple of years helped me cut down on working overtime at my job, and since it was just me in the house since my ex was gone, I made ends meet. Plus, I could spend more time with my cats.

The first road trip I took with my brother wasn't very long, but I was scared. I was seven years old, and Bub was twelve. We had planned a day of fishing and swimming at a local creek with our dad and some of his friends. My dad was still drinking heavily. He got too drunk to drive us home, so he told my brother to drive. The trip was only four or five miles, but I was terrified. Bub was so small, I don't know how he even saw over the steering wheel, let alone reached the pedals. Not that I could see anything anyway. I was crouched down on the floor of the back seat, my head down and my hands covering it, just like they taught us in school for tornado drills back then. Bub, though, as usual, was not scared. He never seemed to be scared. He just took control and got us home safely. Even at twelve, he was nonchalant about the entire thing.

A quick anecdote from a road trip we took around 1996 (I'm not sure where we were going or what we were doing, though; I only remember one thing that happened during it): We were listening to his tape player. He had Guns N' Roses playing, my favorite band from a very early time in my life. The song they covered from the band Rose Tattoo was called "Nice Boys (Don't Play Rock 'n' Roll)." Out of the blue and in perfect rhythm and time with the song, I blurted out, "Nice boys don't tongue the hole." I'm not sure I ever saw him laugh so hard as he did when I said that. He told me afterward, "You could make a living like Weird Al."

In 2001, we took our longest road trip together. Florida. In August. It was oppressively hot. He didn't care. He loved the heat and the beach. I, on the other hand, am made for indoors and air conditioning.

I remember clearly starting out. He and our mom had gone and gotten us a bunch of snacks and stuff to make sandwiches with. On the way, we took a somewhat scenic route. Bub loved road trips. He had a huge road atlas stuffed into the back pocket of his passenger seat everywhere he went. I often wonder how he would feel about modern technology and GPS systems. I have a feeling he would want to stick to his old, trusty atlas.

He planned the entire trip out, every road we would take, places we would stop, and the things we would see on the way. The first place we stopped was the New River Gorge Bridge in West Virginia. I remember we parked, got out of the car. It felt so good to stretch my legs, remembering that we still had something like twelve to fourteen hours of driving ahead of us. Then we walked down a path and around a bend to a lookout that overlooked the gorge. My stomach dropped. I couldn't believe how deep it went. I grabbed the railing for dear life. I thought I was going to fall over, even though that was nearly impossible. Bub walked to the edge and looked down, fascinated. He contemplated what it would be like to bungee jump from the bridge. I told him, "That's something you will have to do without me." He laughed. Then we went and made some sandwiches, ate them, and continued our journey.

One other quick note on the trip down. It saddens me to think about this now, considering how his life played out afterwards. We were driving through a small Florida town. I don't remember now what it was called. There was a foggy, dreary, misting kind of annoying rain going on. We were getting tired. Bub was still driving because, well, he wouldn't let me drive. He rolled through a stop sign. Not a big deal, really, because no one was around. No other traffic. Somehow, a cop neither of us had spotted saw us. He drove up behind us, lights flashing, and pulled us over. Bub gave him his license and asked why he pulled us over. He said he rolled through the stop sign. He took all the information back to his cruiser. Bub said to me, "I hope my license doesn't get suspended."

The cop came back and said everything checked out and because Bub was from out of state, he was just going to let him go with a warning.

Years later, I was thinking on this incident. At the time, I didn't know why Bub was worried his license would be suspended. I knew he had gotten a DUI in Ohio a year or two before. I distinctly recall him calling at something like six a.m.

"Mom, I fucked up. I got a DUI. Love you. Bye."

Like I was saying, I didn't know why he was worried about his license getting suspended. One DUI plus a simple traffic violation wouldn't have resulted in suspension. Years later, it occurred to me it was most likely because he had gotten another DUI, this one in Pennsylvania, and probably not all that long before our trip. He told us about it eventually, but at the time we were stopped in Florida, I didn't know. The license he gave the officer was from Pennsylvania.

We finally made it to Orlando, where our dad's brother Ted lived. He was who we were staying with. We mostly just ventured out during the day and went to the coast. I think we went to three or four different beaches that week. They don't stick out particularly well in my mind because I'm not made for that kind of heat.

One thing that sticks out particularly vivid in my memory, though, happened at Universal Studios. We didn't go into the park; we couldn't afford tickets. We did, however, visit the CityWalk because Bub wanted to go to the Bob Marley bar. He loved Bob Marley's music and was extremely excited to go.

We spent the entire day there. Like beaches, bars are not really for me. I was kind of—hell, I was extremely bored. I don't hate Marley's music, but reggae doesn't really do all that much for me. Bub, however, was having a blast. And he kept drinking and drinking and drinking. He got extremely drunk. When we finally left, after it got dark, I wouldn't let him drive us home. I did not know how to get back to Uncle Ted's house. I have a pretty good sense of direction and can usually navigate to a place once I've driven it once, but this was the first time on the trip Bub had let me drive.

I'm trying to concentrate and find landmarks in a city I know nothing about. We are driving over a bridge or overpass; no other cars are out anywhere. Suddenly Bub says, "I gotta take a piss."

I respond with, "You're going to have to hold it. There's nowhere to go here."

He says back, a little more aggressively, "Pull over. I gotta piss."

I say, "No!"

He says, "Pull over now so I can take a piss, or I'm going to kick your fucking ass!" This was probably the only time in my life my brother spoke to me like this.

I pulled over. He took his piss. I got us back to our uncle's house. He collapsed and passed out on the bed he was sleeping in, still in his clothes and shoes.

The next morning, Uncle Ted said to me, "Smells like someone had too much to drink last night."

"Yeah, definitely," I said.

I remember one time when my parents and I lived in Connecticut, and Mom and I were coming back from visiting Bub in Pennsylvania. My mom was driving her blue Pontiac Sunfire. Great little car. It was a nice, bright sunny day. There was this sportscar that kept playing with us. They would pass us, then slow down, and then Mom would pass them. This went on for almost all of Pennsylvania. And if you have ever driven across Pennsylvania on I-80, it seems like it takes a month. At one point mom was going close to ninety, having just passed them again.

Then, almost immediately, we passed a state highway patrol car. He just shook his finger at us and laughed. Mom didn't slow down.

Another time I was driving, coming down I-95 through New York City. It seemed like just another one of those typical mornings in New York City, the kind of day where you just want to get home and take a nap. It was my first time driving in New York City rush hour traffic. I somehow got into the far-left lane and got pushed; cars were right on my bumper, flashing their lights and blowing their horns. We were doing seventy-plus in damn near bumper-to-bumper traffic. I was scared out of my mind.

I mentioned that Bub did some jail time after his DUI. After he was released from jail and was out of work, my dad and I were taking some food and stuff up to him. This was after a giant snowstorm. We were going to take the Pennsylvania Turnpike, but during the storm there had been something like an eighty-car pileup, and the turnpike was shut down. We ended up having to take back roads in the mountains in central Pennsylvania. I didn't think we were ever going to find our way. We kept calling Bub, and he was trying to give us directions, but every major highway was closed. We ended up taking many two-lane roads until we found our way north to I-80.

My friend Dan and I have been friends ever since kindergarten, when I looked at him and said, "You're tall." (He was then, and he still is to this day.) We have been pretty much inseparable since then. So, some of my adventures with my brother by blood included my brother by circumstance.

A couple of times, we three went to a Pirates game together. On one of them, the Pirates were playing at home. Bub drove because he was the one with the license. I was sitting in the back seat. Dan was riding shotgun. We were jamming to my brother's tunes, probably some heavy metal or something, when suddenly Bub reached up and turned down the radio, then calmly said, "We lost our brakes."

This certainly was not a good thing, because at this precise time we were going down the hill from Greentree to the Fort Pitt Tunnel. If you have ever been down this hill, you know it is steep, it is long, and there are a couple of decently sharp turns on it. It is dangerous enough to necessitate a runaway truck sandpile at the bottom to help big trucks stop if they lose their brakes.

Bub completely kept his calm, though. He said, "Hold on."

We were in a shit-brown Dodge Omni five-speed. Bub went from fifth gear to second in a blink of an eye, and that stopped that shit-brown car faster than a double dose of Kaopectate. I was in the back seat, and I went flying and slammed against the front seat. Dan, in the front passenger seat, slid forward; luckily, he had his seatbelt on. Bub then calmly kept driving. We went to the game, an apparently unremarkable one because I don't recall anything about it. Then Bub drove us home, still with almost no brakes, just smoothly and calmly using his gears and the emergency brake to slow us down and stop us as needed. He never seemed to panic. I never saw him in a situation that seemed beyond his control. I was in awe of him then and remain so to this day.

Perhaps the most fun the three of us had on a trip together was in 2000, when we decided on the spur of the moment to go to a Pirates game yet again, only this time it was in Philadelphia. I made the following Facebook post about it in 2018.

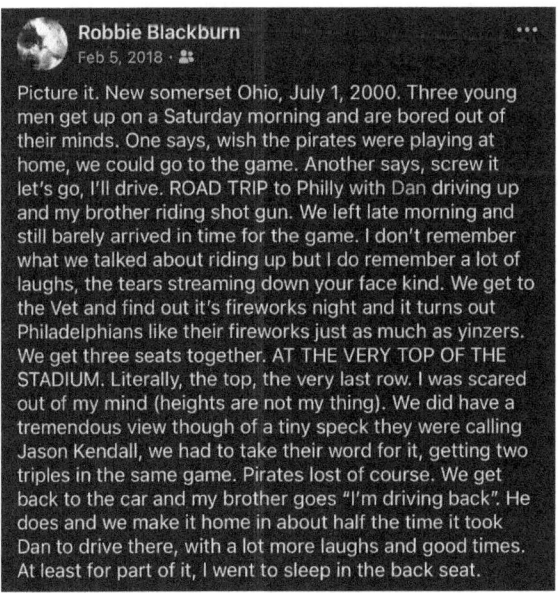

Robbie Blackburn
Feb 5, 2018 ·

Picture it. New somerset Ohio, July 1, 2000. Three young men get up on a Saturday morning and are bored out of their minds. One says, wish the pirates were playing at home, we could go to the game. Another says, screw it let's go, I'll drive. ROAD TRIP to Philly with Dan driving up and my brother riding shot gun. We left late morning and still barely arrived in time for the game. I don't remember what we talked about riding up but I do remember a lot of laughs, the tears streaming down your face kind. We get to the Vet and find out it's fireworks night and it turns out Philadelphians like their fireworks just as much as yinzers. We get three seats together. AT THE VERY TOP OF THE STADIUM. Literally, the top, the very last row. I was scared out of my mind (heights are not my thing). We did have a tremendous view though of a tiny speck they were calling Jason Kendall, we had to take their word for it, getting two triples in the same game. Pirates lost of course. We get back to the car and my brother goes "I'm driving back". He does and we make it home in about half the time it took Dan to drive there, with a lot more laughs and good times. At least for part of it, I went to sleep in the back seat.

While the love of fireworks may be universal across the great commonwealth of Pennsylvania, the attention to detail and the quality certainly are not. The fireworks at Pirates home games were better. Way better. Philly's fireworks lasted maybe ten minutes. As we are walking out, once again Dan is on his bullshit, yelling, "McClatchey spends way more on fireworks than the Phillies. Pirates are way better!" Kevin McClatchey was the principal owner of the Pirates. Some Philadelphians took offense, and I thought once again we were about to get our asses kicked because Dan has a big mouth.

Another example of Bub keeping cool under pressure: I guess this could be called a road trip; we were on a road, and it was certainly a trip of sorts. We were going to Irondale from Hammondsville to play home run derby at the park. As we are going, Bub drives faster, faster and faster. It is a back county road, not the best maintained, twisty, bumpy, and wide enough for two cars and not much more. He looks over at me and says, "The accelerator is stuck." Calm as could be.

I start to panic, knowing there is a sharp turn coming up and at this point we are doing about fifty miles an hour. There is no way he's going to make the turn. He just calmly put the car in neutral (this car was an automatic). The engine is racing, sounds like it is going to blow up. Bub turns off the car and stops us, looks over at me, and says, "Guess we aren't playing home run derby today."

I swear his heartbeat probably didn't top seventy-five, while mine was redlining. I was seeing spots in front of my eyes, felt like I was going to pass out.

The worst road trip ever was one my dad and I made in honor of Bub in 2009. Dad had built a marker to mark the spot where the accident happened, and we drove to Wisconsin to place it. We put it roughly where Bub ended up. I don't know if it is still there or not. I somehow doubt that it is, because we placed it just off the tracks. I doubt whatever entity controls the area around tracks would allow it to stay. The important thing, though, is that we placed it, and in our hearts, it is still there. So, if we never find out any different, then it will be there for all time.

CHAPTER 9

A Dog Called Frog

I wish I could say that I was the first person in my family to write a story, Bub was the first with that as well. In second, maybe third grade, he wrote a story called "A Dog Named Frog." It is an amazing and coherent piece for such a young person to have written. My brother was amazing; I miss him. When my mom found this story so I could add it here, tears welled in my eyes, then spilled over and rolled down my cheeks. I'm making no effort to wipe them away. They streak my face with their heat, leaving behind the burning and yearning to see and hear him one more time. So, without further ado, I present to you the first story written by a Blackburn brother. I am typing it in here with modest edits. After this I will add a photo of it in its original unedited form, straight from the fingers of my brother as a child to your eyes.

A DOG CALLED FROG
BY
JERRY BLACKBURN, JR.

I am at home alone while the Blacks went to the movies. All of a sudden they are barging through the door. As usual they said, "Hi Frog, how were you while we were gone?" Then I saw a kitten in Mrs. Black's hand. They showed me the kitten. "Look what just joined the family," said Mr. Black. "His name is Blackie," said John and Lisa. "Isn't he cute," said Lisa. I barked and thought they knew what I meant.

Then they went into the kitchen and sat the kitten on the floor. Mrs. Black got a bowl and put some cat food in it. Then I came in the kitchen. Mr. Black sat at the table, and I walked over to him. He started petting me and then said, "John, why don't you get

Frog some dog food?" "OK," said John. He got me some dog food and sat it on the floor. While I was eating, I felt something playing with my tail. I turned around and the kitten was playing with my tail. John and Lisa were laughing so hard they couldn't breathe. Mrs. Black had to hit them on the back. I thought I should play too, so I started to wiggle my tail for the kitten to chase.

Then Mr. Black took the kitten into the living room and put him in the basket. I followed him in and laid down beside the basket. Then the rest of the family came into the living room. "You better take good care of Blackie or you will go outside and never be allowed in the house again," said the Blacks together. They all went upstairs to get ready for bed.

While they were in bed I got up and went into the kitchen, and when I came back out the kitten was gone! I walked over to its basket. All of a sudden something jumped out at me. I ran and hid behind the chair. The kitten came walking over to see what was the matter. I said, "You dirty little rascal." All he did was meow. Blackie walked over to his basket in a happy way. I walked over and growled and laid down beside him.

The next morning Mr. Black got up to go to work. Then John and Lisa got up to go to school. John was in the fifth grade and Lisa was in the third. They ate their breakfast. Then they packed their lunches, and then they went to their bus stop. Mrs. Black whistled for me. I went into the kitchen and she laid my bowl down on the floor. She went upstairs to clean the house. When I got done I went into the living room and laid down and went to sleep.

When I woke up, Mr. Black came into the door. He said, "Julie, will you fix me a sandwich?" "OK," said Mrs. Black. Then ten minutes later John and Lisa came running in the door with happy faces. They put their coats in the closet and put their lunch boxes on the kitchen table. Then they went upstairs to change their clothes. When they got done they went outside and called for me to come too. I went outside to see what they wanted. John got a stick and threw it and said, "Fetch, Frog, go get it." When they came in, they took a bath. When they finished, they had some cookies and milk. Then they went to bed at 9 o'clock, and at 10 o'clock Mr. and Mrs. Black went to bed.

In the morning at 6 o'clock I woke up and looked in the basket. The kitten was gone. The one thing to do was to bark, so I barked. Mr. Black came downstairs and said, "What is it, Frog, is there something wrong?" I looked at the basket. "Oh no, Blackie is missing," shouted Mr. Black. John and Lisa came running down the steps. "Blackie is missing," they shouted. "Yes," said Mr. Black. They started to look around the living room. John looked under the couch. Lisa looked under the chair. Mr. Black looked under the television. "He's not anywhere," said Mr. Black.

I went into the kitchen. There he was. His tail was stuck in the cupboard door. I barked and everybody came in the kitchen. "There he is," said Lisa. "Oh Frog, how can we thank you?" said Mrs. Black. "I know how," said Lisa, "we can take him to Grandma's house tomorrow when we go."

The next day, we went to Grandma's house. That's where my mother lives. When we got there, as soon as Mr. Black opened the door I jumped out and ran over to my mother. We barked with happy barks. My mother's name is Rosey. She barked for me to come to meet my Dad. His name is Frisky. "Hi Dad," I said. "How are you doing?" "Fine," he said. Then the Blacks went into the house. While we were outside, they were eating. Then my dad started to play. We chased each other.

At 8 o'clock, I had to go home. When we got there, I went into the house and laid down on the rug. When I woke up in the morning, everyone was gone. I went upstairs, but nobody was in their beds. When I came back downstairs they came out of the kitchen and said, "Happy Birthday, Frog." They sat the cake on the table, and Mrs. Black cut the cake. She gave me the piece with the four on it. Then she cut pieces for rest of the family. Then Grandma came in the door and said, "Surprise, tricked you, didn't I?" Mrs. Black gave Grandma a piece of my birthday cake.

Then they sang, "Happy birthday to you, happy birthday to you, happy birthday dear Frog, our dog, happy birthday to you." At 10 o'clock, Grandma went home. John and Lisa went to bed, and so did Mr. and Mrs. Black.

The next morning, everyone got up with happy smiles on their faces. John said, "How was your birthday party?" I barked. Well, that's the only thing I can do. That night at 6 o'clock, everyone got togther and played five games of Life. John and Lisa went to bed at 11 o'clock. Mr. and Mrs. Black went to bed at 12 o'clock.

Well, that's the end of my story about me and my family. I hoped you liked it, because I enjoyed telling you about us.

THE END

BY

JERRY BLACKBURN, JR.

A DOG CALLED FROG

I am at home alone. While the Black's went to the movies. All of a sudden th
barging through the door. As usual they said "Hi Frog", how were you while we wher
gone?" Then I saw a kitten in Mrs. Black's hand. They showed me the kitten and sa
"look what just joined the family," said Mr. Black. His name is "Blackie", said Jol
and Lisa. "Isn't he cute," said Lisa. I barked and thought they knew what I meant.
Then they went into the kithen and sat the kitten on the floor. Mrs. Black got a bov
and put some cat food in it. Then I came in the kitchen. Mr. Black sat at the tabl
and I walked over to him, he started petting me and then said, "John why don't you
get Frog some dog food?" OK, said John. He got me some dog food and sat it on the
floor. While I was eating , I felt something playing with my tail. I turned around
and the kitten was playing with my tail. John and Lisa were laughing so hard they
couldn't breathe. Mrs. Black had to hit them on the back. I thought I should play
too, so I started to wiggle my tail for the kitten to chase. Then Mr. Black tood t
kitten into the living room and put in the basket. I followed him in and layed dow
beside the basket. Then the rest of the family came into the living room. "You he
take good care of Blackie or you will go outside and never be allowed in the house
again," said the Blacks together. They all went upstairs to get ready for bed. Wl
they were in bed I got up and went into the kichen, and when I came back out the kit
was gone! I walked over to its basket, all of a sudden something jumped out at me.
I ran and hid behind the chair. The kitten came walking to see what was the matter

The original typewritten manuscript of my brother's story "A Dog Called Frog."

CHAPTER 10

The Last Blackburn

I wrote this poem about eleven years ago. I was sitting and thinking about my brother. Also, I was thinking about my grandma, my dad's mom, who passed away in 2011.

THE LAST OF MY NAME

Started out with
Such an inappropriate laugh
You'd think my mind had cracked
It fricked and fracked
Sanity so far from a path
It's gone and lost track
Ticked and tacked
As time ticked and tocked
Therapy was suggested
But I balked
Went and just sat
I could talk
Epic circles cast
Words and words
And more words
But never mentioning the past
Like Roland
I am the last
At least in name only
Once I'm dead and gone
That'll be it, it's all done

There'll be no stories to carry on
Just how the west was won
I may be shunned
Or be the anti hero
None of these outcomes
Is what I fear though
Yet I can't find the words
Words or more words
To bring my fear lighting
I've tried hundreds of times
Writing thousands of lines
As tears flow
In the dead of night.

Near the end of her life, my grandma asked me if I planned to have kids.

I told her, "No, I've never wanted them. Never really considered them. Audrey doesn't want any either."

She begged me on her deathbed to reconsider. I told her I would, but I didn't. I knew from the age of ten that I didn't want kids. My family is vast. I have eleven aunts and uncles just on my mom's side of the family, and all but one of them have kids of their own. I didn't want them.

When my brother died in 2008, that left me as the last Blackburn. I am the end of the line. When I die, our name dies with me. It is a tremendous amount of pressure. There is always a tremendous amount of guilt associated with it as well. Our name goes back a long way, to its origin in Blackburn, England. A side note here: When I was in elementary school and we learned that most last names were originally based on the family's trade, such as blacksmiths having the last name Smith, I feared my ancestors burned black people. Silly where a kid's mind goes.

When my brother died at the age of thirty-two, he had no kids. I can't say for certain that he ever wanted kids, so even if he hadn't died when he did, the name probably would have died with us.

I'm now forty-four and remarried, and I still don't want any kids, and I have no plans to change that. People tell me all the time the joys of having them. When people talk about what gives them joy, those things do not sound good to me. I feel like a lot of times they would be like a drag anchor to me, not merely a detriment which is an obstacle, but the anchor that catches hold and keeps you in place. That is my take on having kids, other who want them then that is fine for them but don't pressure me to live your desired life.

Over the years, even the extended family has been a source of pressure to have a son to carry on the name, but, like I said, I don't want to. My dad's brother attempted to have a son years after he had his single daughter. His wife had her tubal ligation reversed, and they conceived two more children, both girls. This shows how important it was to them that someone carry on the Blackburn name; unfortunately it is just not going to happen. It is a burden I bear. There are many of these; this is just one more. I live with it.

My brother was offered the farm, though. Grandpap Blackburn had put in his will that it be kept in the family. My grandma offered it to him. He refused it. However, I was not offered it. Part of me thought the Blackburn legacy wasn't all that important to everyone in the late '90s. So, in 2011, I was not that worried about it, either. I hate that society as a whole puts pressure on people to have kids. It is no one's fucking business, but they all make it their business. Always telling me what I am missing out on, that there is nothing like having kids. Not having kids is pretty fucking sweet, too, though.

CHAPTER 11

The Cats

Animals. Animals. Animals. My brother loved animals. Our entire family does. Mostly it is cats, but we've had our share of dogs over the years as well. Not to mention we grew up next to our grandparents' farm, so we interacted with cows a lot, too, even had a few as pets over the years. The first cat I recall having was a tortie named Billy Jo. Believe me when I say tortitude is real. She was mostly mean, but she loved Bub. I can recall her snuggling up with him, especially in the car on the way home when we were moving back from New Orleans. After she crossed the rainbow bridge, we went a few years without having a cat. One day, however, my dad, who at the time worked for a couple on their farm, brought home a long-haired calico that we named Missy. Bub and I fought over who would be her "owner." In the end, though, she picked him. She would cuddle up with him all the time.

Missy gave us a lot of kittens, a lot of them. Even though we were habitual watchers of *The Price is Right*, we didn't heed Bob Barker's advice to control the pet population by having our pets spayed or neutered. One kitten Missy had was an orange boy. He was born in 1989, in the summer. Bub laid claim to him immediately. He did, however, have trouble coming up with a name for him. It was days, perhaps even weeks, before he named him. I wanted him to be named Rod, after Rod Woodson, a cornerback for the Steelers. Every time I walked past Bub's room, I would do a little shimmy and shake dance and sing "Hot Rod! Hot Rod! Hot Rod!" Apparently, my dance won him over. Either that, or he accepted my suggestion just to shut me up. Either way, I won the naming contest!

Missy also gave me the cat that became my baby, a pure white kitten named Nike. She loved me from the first time I held her. She only loved me and my mom. Mostly, though, I think that was because my brother used to pick her up and act like he was playing the guitar on her. He called it "Nike Air Guitar." Nike, of course, hated this. She also hated that he called her Reebok. Then, as happens so often with pets, her nickname became Niker-Bok. She disappeared one day and never came home. It wasn't until my brother and I were at a party in 2003 that I found out what happened to her. He told me that my mom found her dead in the neighbor's yard. It looked like she had been poisoned.

I'm not going in chronological order as to when we had each cat. We had a lot of them over the years (again, sorry, Bob). However, if I had to name the cat that was my brother's favorite when we were kids, it would unquestionably be TP, named for Tony Peña, who was the catcher for the Pirates. TP was born to my Aunt Eunice's cat. The mother rejected him, so my family adopted him, and our mom bottle-fed him cow's milk. This was in the mid-1980s; I don't know if there was kitten supplement milk then or not. TP survived, but he became a milk fiend. Bub always got up early and ate a bowl of cereal for breakfast, studying the back of the cereal box while he ate. (Side note: One of his favorite cereals was Cap'n Crunch, which I hated; that shit was way too hard. It always hurt the roof of my mouth.) Me, on the other hand, I slept as long as I could and rarely ate breakfast. Some things never change. Anyway, Bub would then drink off most of the milk that was left in the cereal bowl, but TP would sit beside his chair and meow, and meow and meow—that cat had a loud, piercing meow—until my brother let him drink off the last bit of his milk. Every morning, without fail, TP drank the last bit of my brother's breakfast cereal milk. It never made him sick, either. TP loved Bub, followed him everywhere he went. He always slept with him at the foot of his bed, sat on him when he sat on the couch, and of course sat beside his chair whenever he ate. Sadly, one day, we were getting in the car to go swimming in the creek close to our house. We were backing up, and my dad heard a thump. TP was under the car. My brother jumped out and grabbed him. TP scratched the shit out of his arm, deep scratches that bled profusely, yet he didn't even seem to feel them. He just sat and held him as he died, looking up into my brother's face, giving one last meow, probably the softest meow ever. It was as if he was saying to him, "Thank you for loving me."

My brother wept. I don't know that I ever in my life saw him cry as hard as he did then. He took TP to the backyard and buried him under a maple tree. The grave to this day still has a stone over it. Over the years, there have been a lot of stones placed in our rainbow graveyard.

We still went swimming. Being a child and not having any couth, I asked my brother, "Are you sad about TP?"—while I was there watching him cry.

One other time I saw my brother cry when we were kids was when our grandma ran over his dog, Snoopy. He wasn't a beagle, but he was still cute. My brother was his person for sure. Snoopy followed him around everywhere. He would always lie right beside him in bed or on the couch. When we would go outside to play, wherever you saw my brother, inside or outside, you were certain to see Snoopy as well. This one day we were outside playing. My parents' house was on top of a hill with a driveway that, as you were going up it, swung out wide to the right. It was probably a few hundred feet long total. Our grandparents' drive veered off to the right and went down into a sort of valley. In between was a wedge of grass and dirt we liked to play on with our toy trucks, shovels, and various other toys. One day when we were playing, our grandma came up the driveway and headed out to the road. Snoopy had been beside us. Some time went by, and we noticed he wasn't there beside us anymore. We saw him lying in their driveway. Bub called for him, but he didn't move. He was dead. Our grandma had run him over. She later told our mom that she knew she had hit something but then kept going. Bub picked Snoopy up and carried him to the house, where he and our mom buried him.

Another cat that we had—this one, we did share—was a pure black fluffy guy that was extremely cuddly. He would alternate who he slept with. Usually it was me, though. I slept with my door open. Because Bub was in his teens by this point, he always slept with his door closed, so this kitty was more likely to sleep on my bed. We named him Al, after Al Martin, an outfielder for the Pirates. Al fathered a few kittens for us. One was born in 1998, a pure black kitten we named Al Jr., or AJ. I wanted to claim AJ, but after I went to Ohio University in the fall of

1998, my brother came home and claimed him, took him to live with him in Pittsburgh, and never gave him back. All was not lost, however. The next year, Al fathered a clone of himself, a kitten we named Al the Third, or, as he became known, Three.

I want to talk more in depth about AJ, but first I'll make a quick note about Three and talk about one that was my mom's baby. After I spent a year at Ohio U, which I hated, I transferred to Mount Union. The second year I was there, in 2001, Three disappeared for a few days. My mom hadn't seen him, my dad went out looking for him, and I was getting worried. I was going to go home on the weekend and look for him. Before I could, though, he came home. The way I found out he was home was a message from my brother on Yahoo Messenger that said, "Your fuckin fur ball is home." He knew I was worried as hell about him, and, with extreme gentleness and tact, he let me know he had come home.

Before Missy passed away, she had a kitten that we named Pity Patty, after our aunt Pat, probably because she was short and chunky. She was one of the fluffiest cats we ever had. She was the first in a long line of black and tan tabby cats. Pity Patty then had a kitten we named Minnie, a black and tan tabby like her mom, except she was always long and skinny unless she was pregnant. Minnie was my mom's baby and AJ's mom. Also, Marty's mom; I will talk about them in a minute. Minnie loved McDonald's french fries. Every year on Mother's Day, my brother would call me and tell me to go get her some french fries from AJ and Marty.

Minnie had many kittens. Long after she should have been past kitten-rearing age, she was still having them. The first, however, was George, a black and gray tabby. There was only the one kitten in her first litter. George was a girl, but we thought she was a boy. My mom insists to this day that her name was Dexter. She even calls the addition on the back of her house "Dexter's room." Bub and I called her George. Sometimes we'd half-ass concede and call her Dexter-George. But George was always in the name. Minnie didn't seem to want George, though. She kept taking her and placing her under my brother's bed, in his track shoes. I imagine they smelled awful. Minnie did this at least three, maybe four times. George was a good little sister to us, though.

She let us pick on her. We used her as a football. My brother or I would hold her like a football in our arms and then try to get across the living room to score a touchdown. George would just lie in our arms. Or we would slide her across the floor like a hockey puck. She was a good sport. She would slide across the floor, then start to run and spin in place for a while and run toward one of us, and we would grab her and slide her back across the floor. It was a great game to play.

My mom and dad got an abused cockatiel from someone my dad knew. His name was Mickey. I swear we didn't plan to have a Mickey and a Minnie in the house, neither of them being a mouse. Bub loved Mickey. Loved that damn bird. He would let him out of his cage all the time. Mickey didn't exactly love being out of his cage; he would be scared, especially if there was a fly buzzing around. He was deathly afraid of bugs. Even if he was in his cage, he would get all the way in the bottom and cuss at the fly, usually saying, "Bastard, Bitch, Dammit." Bub may or may not have been the one to teach him those words. He also taught him another phrase. Bub loved to play the games in the Medal of Honor franchise, especially the one for PlayStation 1 set in Germany. He would get Mickey's cage and let him out and yell to him, "Hey Mick, wanna kill kraut?" Eventually Mickey started to ask him, "Kill Kraut?" Well, really, he asked everybody if they wanted to kill kraut. One other thing Bub taught him, which drove our mom nuts, was "Mom" and "Mommy." Every time Mickey would see my mom, he would say "Mommy" or "Mom." One time my mom came home from work when Bub had let Mickey out of his cage on their enclosed porch. Bub must have forgotten about him and then taken a nap. When my mom got home, all she heard was a real soft "Mommy" from up in the corner of the porch. Mickey was hanging onto the wall and begging for help.

Bub always wanted a Siberian husky, but that was one dream that never came to fruition for him. He loved dogs, though, all dogs. One he especially loved was my mom's and dad's Pomeranian, named Coco. One of my friends found Coco in Alliance, Ohio. He went to a couple days of college classes until he found his forever home with us. Bub would play with that dog for hours, and Coco loved him.

I keep putting off going into detail about my brother's absolute babies, AJ and Marty, I think because it hurts too much to think about them. After Bub died, they were the last living links to him besides family. In the spirit, though, I'll tell you about Minnie's last litter of kittens. She had a clone we named Sarah. Sarah had a kitten we never knew where he came from. We named him Sammy. Sammy looked white when he was born. Not long after that, he turned darker. Then, as he grew, he changed from dark to light with the seasons. He also had the biggest, brightest blue eyes you ever saw. My brother tried to claim him, but he wasn't leaving my mom. Sammy was her baby. She had let Bub claim one of her babies before. It would not happen again.

That baby was Marty. Marty was the ultra-rare male calico cat. While almost all male calico cats are sterile, Marty was not. He fathered three babies. My brother named them Mini Mart, UniMart, and Dairy Mart. Only the Mini Mart name stuck. UniMart became Cody, and Dairy Mart, ironically, became Ralph, like Ralph the cat from a WDVE radio skit. Ralph, and here's the irony, loved milk. He loved the kitten supplement milk. He loved the milk treats, and he loved the dry cat food they used to have that had milk chunks in it. Cody was really smart and could open anything. He would open the bags of the food, and Ralph would pull out the pieces of the milk and leave the kibble alone.

Back to Marty, though. My brother was living in Connecticut, and my mom and dad were taking AJ up to him, since had an apartment (one that he hated; I'll talk about that apartment in another chapter). My mom and dad had to take Marty along on that trip because he was just a baby and he had to be bottle-fed. They also took George because she was a princess and couldn't be left home alone. As soon as my brother saw Marty, he said, "He's staying here." He stayed there. Bub took over bottle-feeding him. From that point on, AJ and Marty were inseparable.

Before Marty came along, though, AJ got into some hijinks on his own. One particular example was when Bub was living with his coworker named Mike. AJ got outside through a screen and took on a skunk. He lost. He came in smelling like its spray. My brother called our mom in the middle of the night, wanting to know how to get the smell off him. AJ smelled like a skunk for weeks afterwards, Bub said.

AJ and Marty were quite the pair. They had a very similar dynamic to Bub and me. AJ, as the older brother, was always the protector. When my brother lived in a condo, he would let them go outside and roam the courtyard. If AJ came back without his brother, Bub would say, "Go get your brother." Then, within a few minutes, they'd both be back at the door, ready to come in the house. They travelled together, too. My brother would come home on some weekends, especially around the holidays, and he always brought the boys with him. He wouldn't leave them there by themselves for that long. AJ did fine in the car. Marty was a nervous rider. Bub always said that within twenty minutes of leaving, Marty would take a shit and stink up the car. Without fail, he would kick litter everywhere as well. I bet that wherever that Mustang is, if it is still rolling the roads of America, there is cat litter in some of those crevices in the back seat.

One time when they came home, AJ came back from outside without Marty, because Marty was still inside and hiding from the trip and hadn't come out yet. I told AJ, "Go get your brother."

He wanted right back outside; he scratched at the door to be let out.

Bub said to me, "Don't tell him that; he will go look for him." Bub ended up having to take AJ to see Marty under the bed where he was hiding.

Bub would always come home for Thanksgiving and bring the boys for an extended stay with Grandma. He would come back at Christmas because his plant shut down for the week between Christmas and New Year's. He would often call and check on them, telling my mom, "You better not be making them soft. I am toughening them up." My mom would claim that she wasn't, but she was. She was giving them treats and petting them. My brother liked to hold them up each in one arm and make them fight. They loved to do it. He would play extremely rough with AJ especially. AJ would scratch the hell out of Bub's arms and hands, but Bub didn't care. Marty eventually acquired the nickname WallyMart, I guess in the same line as the store names Bub gave the kittens Marty fathered. He couldn't deny the kittens; they all had his white-tipped tail. Two of my favorite pictures of my brother are of him holding AJ and Marty. I have them both framed in my house. The one with AJ I had made into a customized blanket for my mom for Christmas in 2010. Below is a picture of the blanket.

The photo blanket I got for my mom for Christmas 2010.

THAT WHICH IS LEFT BEHIND

When I woke up this morning
I didn't plan on dying
I'm sorry my number was called
And that you are now crying
I hate that I'll never finish that book
I don't know if I can forgive myself
For the vacations I never took
I wish I would have taken more time to relax
Maybe it would mean I'd still be alive, perhaps
I wonder where it goes
All the time that we have wasted
Maybe boredom is just another name for those
Times life has us hastened
I regret the news you've been informed
It was never my intention
To have your life's normalcy torn
From my name's mention
To have so many touching eulogies performed
In my honor
Maybe I should have never gone there
But in the end, our decisions are made
The price is paid
The path is laid
And we go about on our way
But I have regrets
And they are plenty
I focused too much on money
I arrived late and left early
I didn't say things that needed to be said
I stayed clean when I should have gotten dirty
I played a victim

When sometimes I was just a fool
I got hot when I should have played it cool
It sucks I'll never get to finish that series
It hurts me to think to myself
That I will be easy to forget
I hate myself a little for leaving behind
So much debt
I'm sorry that I left my house a mess
Who will explain it to my cats
About my death?

The above poem doesn't fit perfectly with my brother's death. I wrote it from my perspective.

No one will ever convince me that our pets don't know when we die. After Bub died, AJ and Marty both appeared to grieve. They would both get on my mom's nightstand and stare at his picture. AJ would often lie down beside it and paw at his face. They know, and we cannot explain it to them. One thing I always hope—because I feel cats and other animals can see into different realms than humans can—is that they can see their loved ones when they pop in for a visit. I think that when you see a cat staring off into a particular area where nothing appears, a loved one is visiting.

Animals' losses are so much harder to see than those of humans, because animals hide it. But they don't always hide it well. For weeks, probably months after Bub's death, AJ and Marty moped around the house. AJ would go to the door and meow. They knew the time of year as well. When Christmas came around, they sensed it. They knew they always saw their daddy at Christmas. When he didn't come, it was like their little hearts broke all over again.

Marty guarding the Christmas presents. We lost
Marty first, on October 16, 2012.

AJ wearing the sweater our mom got for him. We lost AJ on January 31, 2016.

CHAPTER 12

Kitchen Stories

Bub liked to cook. Not always foods I necessarily liked to eat, but he did like to cook. As a bachelor, it came with the territory, I guess: he had to either learn to cook or eat out every day. He wouldn't have eaten out every day. He was a frugal person mostly. If he were alive today, he would still have a flip phone and he'd refuse to text even though texting is free now. Back then he refused to text because he didn't want to pay for it. I received one text message from him in his life. It was on New Year's Eve of 2007–'08, and it read simply "HAPPY NEW YEAR". Unfortunately, 2008 was not a happy year; it was in fact a terrible year. The shitstorm started in January. My wife at the time, Audrey, worked at a shoe store and got robbed at "gunpoint", which turned out to be the guy's finger in his pocket. In February, obviously, came what happened with my brother, and in March, Audrey hit a patch of ice and wrecked. So yeah, not a good year. Not that I believe my brother's lone text message to me caused any of this; it's just a bitter irony is all.

Back to his cooking, though. When we were growing up, Friday was always pizza day. We loved to make our own pizzas, and we always used Chef Boyardee pizza kits. I'd get to make my own the way I liked it, which was a bunch of cheese and meats. Bub wasted his pizza by adding vegetables to it. We always competed as to whose pizza was better. I, of course, always won because I'm the better cook. Or so I always told myself.

I remember one of the first times he cooked for me after he moved out and was living on his own. He made us what we called "poor man's food." I don't know what the actual name is; I've heard some people call it shit on a shingle. I guess maybe the name for it is regional. We called it poor man's food. It was supposed to be fried potatoes, eggs, and sausage mixed. We'd watched our mom make it for years. She would fry the sausage first, then add the other stuff. Well, Bub decided to use ground beef instead of sausage. We never saw our mom drain the grease off the sausage, so Bub didn't drain the grease off the ground beef. It was a greasy mess. I still ate it. Then, predictably, I got sick with diarrhea. Which Bub thought was pretty funny. He was used to his own cooking; I guess it didn't affect him the same way it did me.

Another cooking misadventure occurred several years later. I wasn't at our parents' house for this one; I only heard the story later. Bub was crazy to try deep-fried turkey for Thanksgiving. So, he bought a turkey fryer and all the stuff needed for the process. He heated the oil to the correct temperature, then dropped the turkey in. It went in a little too fast, because the oil splashed out everywhere, setting the fryer and the surrounding grass on fire. Surprisingly, the turkey stayed in the fryer and remained cookable. I showed up later; the turkey was delicious, and it was a funny story for all the rest of time.

One reason I did not care for my brother's cooking was his desire to make everything as hot as possible. We both have our trademarks when it comes to cooking. Mine is that I add pepperoni to just about everything. His trademark was to add peppers, most notably jalapeños. I remember one time he made chili at his place in Connecticut, then transported it all the way back to Ohio. Our dad loves chili. He got a bowl, added his crackers, took a bite, and screamed, "Holy fuck that's hot!"

Bub laughed, then said, "Yeah, it's not bad. I added jalapeños. Just dumped the entire jar in, juice and all."

Dad was always careful when he would eat Bub's chili ever after.

CHAPTER 13

Movies

Bub loved movies. He had an extensive collection of DVDs when he died, despite having gone on a spree of selling his movies to get a few bucks to get food and pay his bills when he was out of work. A few movies that were on his no-sell list were ones he would often quote, and on a slow day he would put them on as background. If he saw one of them on TV, he would invariably stop and watch the rest of it. If he had a list of his top ten favorite movies, I'm not sure I would know the order of them all, but I know what number one would be: *Star Wars*. He loved all the Star Wars movies, even the prequel trilogy, which for a lot of Star Wars fans may be considered blasphemy. He didn't care, though. That galaxy far, far away was just something he loved. It saddens me so much that he isn't here to see all the new movies and series that have come out and are still to come out in the intervening years since his death. Think whatever you will about the newer ones and their potential flaws; I know he would have loved them all. That hit me when I went to the theater the day Episode 9, *The Rise of Skywalker*, came out. I thought that it was going to be the last of the primary arc of the franchise. As we know, there have been several offshoots and series and spinoffs of the major movies, but this was going to be the last. We now know this may not be the case.

But I digress. I watched the movie by myself at the "midnight showing" the day before the release. The reason for the quotes is that the showing was at 6:00 pm. I'm so glad I watched it in 3D and had the glasses on, because I cried the entire movie. I just leaked at the eyes. And then, when we thought Chewie got blown up, I openly wept. Chewie was always one of my brother's favorite characters. He and C3PO. I hope that if there is a heaven, and I believe there is one, that some of the earthly endeavors we loved can still be accessed, and that Bub has gotten the opportunity to watch these movies. He was with me, though, in the theater. I watched it at a luxury theater that had recliner seats with tables. I sat him on the little table right beside my popcorn and his nachos, which he got everywhere he went. Whether it was baseball, football, or the movies, he always got nachos.

In no particular order, I'll list some of his other favorite movies.

First is *Animal House*. He saw that movie a hundred times, but he never failed to laugh really hard at it. When I first watched it with him, I was not overly impressed. I thought it was kind of dumb. However, it has grown on me over the years, and it is now one of my favorite movies.

A movie we rented and watched together back in the early '90s that we both loved from the first is *Dazed and Confused*. It is a masterpiece of a film: funny, poignant, and overall just a great movie. For days after watching it, we would walk around going, "Alright, alright, alright." I think another aspect of the movie that drew us in was the fact that the primary bully in the movie, Ben Affleck's character, loses in the end. He gets a bucket of paint dropped on him. Bub and I were both bullied in school, and it felt good to live vicariously through the bullied character. Not to mention, holy shit, that fucking soundtrack is to die for. Chef's kiss.

My mom will hate that I'm talking about this next one because she hates it so much. Bub? He loved it. Loved it. Loved it. *A Christmas Story*. He loved that movie so much. I don't know how else to explain it. Back when he was alive, TNT or TBS—I can't remember which, because they both do it now—would run *A Christmas Story* twenty-four hours straight on Christmas Day. One year, Bub put it on and then hid the remote so we ended up having to have it on all day because we had the type of cable box that only a remote could control. He laughed at how mad our mom got. To this day, if you mention it around her she will immediately say, "I hate that show."

Another Christmas movie that Bub always watched, multiple times every year, was *National Lampoon's Christmas Vacation*. He loved all the *Vacation* movies, but that one especially. His love has been transferred to me. I now watch it multiple times a year, and not just at Christmas. My wife and I watch it all year long.

A lot of the movies that Bub loved had strong soundtracks or were musical types of movies. One he absolutely loved—I'm not even a hundred percent sure what genre it would fall into—was *The Blues Brothers.* He loved that movie so much. I think now, looking back at some movies he loved, maybe he just loved John Belushi.

Another movie he could probably have played all day long without problems is *Pink Floyd—The Wall.* I remember the first time I watched it. I was staying with Bub at his apartment in Pittsburgh. Pink Floyd's music always appealed to me, but this movie took it to another level. Seeing a movie that created the scenes from the songs blew my teenage mind. After it was over, he looked at me and went, "Pretty good, huh?"

Absolutely, Bub. Absolutely.

Absolutely one of his top ten all-time favorites was *Cool Hand Luke.* He loved that movie. Loved it long before Guns N' Roses put it back in the national consciousness with their song "Civil War," which opens with a sample of Strother Martin's famous line "What we have here is a failure to communicate." I remember fairly well the details of the day I first saw it, even though I was probably only eight. My mom was going to a sort of night school. So, our dad took us to this small video rental place in Toronto. It was our second most frequent video rental destination after Blockbuster Video. My dad picked up *Cool Hand Luke* and said, "This one is pretty good." We rented it. We always balanced a drama with a comedy, and I believe the other one we rented was either *Short Circuit* or *Revenge of the Nerds.* Dad was right. Even at the age I was, Paul Newman's character was a marvel to behold. For me, it was the idea that the main character was a "bad guy" because most of society teaches us that only bad people go to jail. Luke was in jail, therefore he had to be bad. He wasn't, though. You could see throughout the movie and even feel it in almost every scene. The man was just sad. A flawed tragic hero type. Perhaps I'm drawn to that type of protagonist. It could explain the love I have for Roland Deschain in the *Dark Tower* series. I know Bub loved it, too, even though we never discussed the why of his loving it. Maybe Dragline describes both Luke and my brother pretty well at the end: "He was smiling. . . . That's right. You know, that, that—that Luke smile of his. He had it on his face right to the very end. Hell, if they didn't know it 'fore, they could tell right then that they weren't e'er gonna beat 'im. That old Luke smile. Oh, Luke. He was some boy. Cool Hand Luke. Hell, he's a natural-born world-shaker." Maybe Bub saw himself as a natural-born world-shaker. He so often had that same sort of smile, a sort of mischievous smirk like, "Sometimes life sucks, but I'm having as much fun as I can right now." That little smirk that fills their blue eyes with light not only lights up their faces, but anyone gazing upon them, it lights up their hearts as well.

If *Star Wars* was number one on Bub's list, I think a close second would be *Forrest Gump*. There are multiple reasons for this, I think. Foremost is the soundtrack. What an amazing soundtrack that movie has. Bub would watch the movie just to hear the songs because, as I seem to recall him saying, the CDs were hard to find. He loved the entire movie: the script, the historic footage, even the incidental music. It was all amazing to him. His favorite part, which is probably my least favorite part of the movie, is when Forrest takes off running and running and running. I think it is dumb. Bub loved it. Said he would love to just run across the country like that. I think part of the reason he loved that scene is that a couple of places they show Forrest running are places Bub visited with our grandparents when he was a kid—most specifically, the lake that was "two skies, one right on top of the other." A bittersweet irony of this movie, if that is the proper term for this, I don't know, is that the running time of the movie is 2 hours and 22 minutes, like 2/22, the day Bub died. This number is everywhere. I will talk more about that later.

A lot of these movies, to this day when I get to missing Bub so much it is palpable, I will put them on. I am so blessed to have a partner in Amanda who not only tolerates this but understands and enjoys them as well. Often, I will put something on to fall asleep to it. It almost feels like I'm staying with him again and we are watching them together, because I know he would be happy to put any of these movies on at any time. With these movies on my TV screen, Bub is almost close enough to touch. The ghost of the memories is given breath and returns to me, breathing back into him a life that was cut tragically short. It gives me a way to create new, fresh memories with him.

CHAPTER 14

Signs from Bub

Two two two. 222. What is it? What does it mean? Is it blue car syndrome? Is it a sign? Is it positive? Is it negative? Am I being fucked with? These are questions I ask myself all the time. I am forced to because I see this number so often in my daily life. I see it on license plates, in phone numbers. I pick up my phone, and so often the time is 2:22. I don't know. I can't explain it. It seems to happen too often to be coincidental. It happens too often for me to not feel like I'm being fucked with. That sort of humor would be right up Bub's alley, too. He would take something I see as tragic and use it to fuck with me. He had a great sense of humor, but sometimes it could border on sadistic. For example, in 2002 or '03, the Steelers were playing the Tennessee Titans in a playoff game. A radio station in Nashville ran a promotion, "Get Tommy Maddox to the hospital" or something like that. See, a few weeks before, Tommy had been knocked out during a game and had to be taken by ambulance from the field to the hospital. The promotion was a race where each two-person team had a gurney and one person had to push the other. Winner won tickets to the game. Bub thought this was hilarious. I thought it was ignorant. So, yeah, his humor could be sadistic. This feels like one of those times.

I think it is a sign from him. I wish I could figure out what it means. Doing research on the spiritual meanings of the number, I have found that people believe that 222 is associated with balance, collaboration, love, and harmony. According to spiritual author Doreen Virtue, 222 means "Trust that everything is working out exactly as it's supposed to, with divine blessings for everyone involved."

I'm not sure will go that far with the meaning that everything is working out as it is supposed to. I don't think my brother was supposed to die how he did. That seems messed up to me. Still, like I said, it feels like

222 appears far too often to just be coincidence. I have a theory: Part of me thinks that Bub would much prefer to present me with the number 666 because it is so often referenced in heavy metal music, which he loved. But it would be difficult for him to make that number show up in my daily life, since clocks don't go to 6:66 and license plates usually avoid 666 because of its connotations. So maybe 222 is his workaround. He certainly uses it as often as he can.

Seeing the number 222 was a trigger for me for a very long time. I hated it. I would get angry. Irrationally so. I thought the universe was mocking me by making me feel the pain repeatedly. Seeing that number was on par with hearing a train's chuff-chuff-chuff or the sound of its whistle. I think my residual anger from the tragedy just worked its way into me. These signs, for want of a better term, constantly reminded me that I felt I was to blame. The pain they triggered was my punishment. It was too hard to think it could be anything else. There is no prison sentence for survivor's guilt except for the prison of your own mind, where you sit looking through the bars of your own thoughts into the darkness of self-loathing, making everything feel just as real on day five thousand or ten thousand as it did on day one. The wound must be kept fresh, because that is what is deserved. Healing never really seems like an option, only festering.

However, over the past few years, Amanda has provided me with a fresh perspective on signs. She takes them as more of a sign that Bub is just checking in. That he is saying "Hi. I'm doing fine. Don't worry about me. I got your back. I'm watching out for you." That sort of thing. Every time she sees the number, she responds, "Hi, Bub."

She has certainly lightened my heart toward the number. I don't hate seeing it anymore. I don't have to convince myself that it is just a number. It's a sign, from him to me, to us, and it has wound its way into the grieving process. It is a tooth on the cog of the wheel of memory, designed to catch and help turn us daily toward the future and the time when we'll meet him once again.

I believe that he sends me signs all the time. Not just the number, which, like I said above, I am uncertain of the full meaning behind. I guess it could truly be all of the above, except the part about the universe punishing me and mocking me.

Another sign that I see very often is the presence of cardinals around me. So often, I will be outside and a cardinal will sing to me. A family of cardinals lives in a nest in my yard. If I sit out on the glider for a while, the male will eventually come out and sit in the tree above my head and sing to me. The female almost always comes out eventually as well. This year, for the first time, they have introduced me to their baby. Just the other day, all three of them were out, singing and walking in my yard.

Something just happened so profound that I can't help but include it in this manuscript. I am sitting in my home office, working through the edits my editor sent me. I had just started revisiting this chapter when I heard a noise outside, a soft fluttering against the window screen. I looked up, and there she was—a female cardinal, clinging to the screen and staring directly at me.

She stayed there for what felt like an eternity, but it couldn't have been more than ten seconds, before climbing out of sight.

I sat there, frozen, staring at the spot where she had been, my breath caught in my chest, mouth open, and tears welling in my eyes.

Sometimes when we're unsure about how we're doing—especially on a project so deeply tied to our emotions—we need confirmation that we're on the right track. I take that female cardinal as a sign, a message from my brother. It feels like his way of saying, *I see you. I'm proud of you. Keep going.*

I have seen cardinals during a few times of trouble. I recall distinctly that when I was trying to recover from my divorce in the summer of 2019, I had gotten to a very low point. I was questioning whether I even need to exist anymore. I felt unloved and unlovable. It was during the road trip I took to Massachusetts. I was sitting outside in a chair, the one outdoor chair the hotel provided, and a male cardinal flew down and sat next to me on the arm of the chair. He sat there for at least five minutes. He just looked at me. Looked into me. I took that inspiration and immediately wrote this:

QUESTIONS AND ANSWERS

What would we do if
We were given an answer
To every question why
What if every tear we ever cried
For reasons that were never a surprise,
What if we had the reason
Behind every lie
How would it feel to know
Everything you ever tried
Would turn out right
What if all the answers
Were kept inside
But we are just too blind
Hiding behind the cliché
That I am fine
What if the truth is within our grasp
But no matter how hard you tried
You just couldn't make it last
It slipped away too fast
Another ship getting under way
Sails at full mast
What if all we had was
Just a little class
Another day gone by
Where we asked
For the reasons why
Just another truth
Inside, yet one more lie
One more deep breath
Shortened to a sigh

One last lonely tear,
That won't turn into a cry
So many questions
That none can answer
Another sleepless night
At least let us shake hands, sir
All these things
I was never meant to know
It's time to just let em go
Nothing good can come
From this mental picture show
Only one more day
Of feeling pretty low
Just need to live life
With all its ebbs and flow,
All those questions why
They can go wherever
Unanswered questions go to die
It's about to be my time
All the world could be mine
All I have to do is try.

After my wordless conversation with that cardinal, I felt I had found some peace with not knowing the answers to all questions that need to be asked. I reached a place where I understood that with some questions, it may ultimately be better to not know the answers.

December 17, 2022 was the day I became the luckiest man on earth and married my beautiful bride, Amanda. Yes, three twos showed up again in that date. But they were a good sign this time, of that I am certain.

As we were getting ready that day, we had taken all the stuff we were taking to the wedding venue out to my car. The car was sitting at an angle to the porch, not where I normally park. I had just gotten out of the shower, and I looked out the window and there was a cardinal sitting on the rear-view mirror. It stayed for a very long time, long enough for me to get a video and pictures of it. One of those pictures is below. I took this cardinal as a sign that Bub was going to attend the wedding. He was the best man at my first wedding, and after he died, I'd always said I would never marry again because my best man was gone. I took this cardinal as a sign that Bub was fine with me getting married again without him being present—not physically, at least. I also took it as a sign that Bub approved of Amanda for me.

A cardinal looking at himself the mirror the day Amanda and I got married. Maybe Bub came for the wedding and needed to check his fit for the event. Had to make sure he was spiffy and prepared. I believe he was.

CHAPTER 15

My Protector

diabetes

As we talked, you need to take care of yourdelf. I know its hard, (trust me l do) but you have to try.

You have at least two people that love you more than the world itself, and anything that would happen to you would be be just too devastating. and i can't live with that. Because I am a role model to you and because of that I try to be the best that I can be, and that is the biggest reason I am where I am today. Don't worry about money, what your insurance won't cover I will, but I plan on being around a long time, and those plans include you.

your brother

* * *

I stated earlier that I would return to the above email in a different context. The earlier context was that it made me angry because of the broken promise he made to me. He did not end up being around for a long time. Here, however, the context is the email's true purpose: to show that he supported me no matter what. He didn't care about the money; he made a good wage as an electrical engineer. With his frugality, he had money put back and could help me. He sent me money a couple of times to cover my diabetic supplies. For the most part I did better, got myself under control, and set myself right.

He supported me in other ways as well. One of the first times I remember him supporting me, protecting me, and being there for me is when I was in first grade and he was in fifth grade. We were riding the bus home from elementary school. There was a sixth grader who kept picking on me. I was sitting there in my seat, crying. Someone alerted Bub to my condition. He waited until the bus made a stop and quickly came up to the seat I was in and asked me, "What's wrong?"

I tried not to answer. He could tell something was wrong, though. I had tears running down my face, snot running from my nose. I couldn't lie to him very well. I told him, "He keeps making fun of me," and I pointed to the kid in the seat across from me. I didn't know who he was then, and I still don't know his name. My brother looked at his friend Jason in the seat behind that kid. Then he jumped over into the kid's seat and elbowed him in the stomach, which bent him over, as he'd had the wind knocked out of him. Bub then elbowed him in the head. Then leaned over and said to him, "You ever say anything to my brother again, you'll get worse from me or the guy behind us."

Jason was a big dude, even in elementary school. He was probably five foot eight, maybe close to 180 pounds, and strong as hell. From that day on, I had two protectors: my brother and Jason. If Bub wasn't around, Jason happily stepped in. Once when a different kid knocked me down during our morning recess and didn't bother to stop and apologize, Jason punched the kid in the head several times and got a detention. He didn't tell the teacher why he'd done it, either; he just accepted the punishment.

I always enjoyed having that sort of protection. Not that I was a troublemaker or a smart-ass to people. But I was poor, I had dark curly hair, and I got the best grades, which was the object of ridicule by the ignorant. There were many times I needed that protection, and I used it.

The protection wasn't limited to physical altercations. Bub protected my mind as well. He was always there to talk to when I needed someone, especially if I was down. Somehow he just seemed to know when I needed a kind word or a kick in the ass. Big-brother instincts, I guess. He was a tremendous confidant, an excellent mentor, and a tough but fair critic. He would tell me what I needed to hear, not what I wanted to hear. After I graduated from college, I was working part time for our uncle Fred. Uncle Fred owns his own trucking company, so I was helping around the garage. I cleaned up, helped work on trucks, made part runs, basically anything that needed to be done and was within my skill set. I did this because I had no confidence that I could transition from college into the adult working world. Bub called me on the phone one day and said, "This is ridiculous that a college graduate is working in a garage sweeping up dirt. Get a real fucking job. I know you can do it." I had confessed to him in a Yahoo Messenger conversation that I was scared. He told me, "You're the smartest person I know. You can do anything. So now go do it."

That night, I got on the internet to apply for a few jobs. The first job I applied for, I got a call back the next day, and I interviewed a few days later. The director seemed impressed with me and offered me a job on the spot. That was the job at Pyramid Healthcare. I was there from October 2003 until April 2004. In February 2004, I attended a training. In that training, someone introduced themselves as the new "counselor here at Hickory Lodge." This dumbfounded me, because I had talked to the director and she had promised me that the new counselor position would be mine when it opened up. She hadn't wanted to hire me into that position because I didn't have any experience, but she promised me that if I continued working there, she would tell me when the next counselor position opened up. But I wasn't even aware that they were hiring anyone. The facility I was working at was brand new. When I started, there were only two residents.

To say that I was fuming would be an understatement. I worked a midnight shift a few nights later. During midnights it was slow, so I could get on the computer at work, and Bub and I chatted on Yahoo Messenger again. I wanted to rage-quit. He talked me out of it, saying that it wouldn't do me any favors for my future endeavors. So I looked for a new job. I found one on the Pennsylvania CareerLink website. It was a company called Sharp Visions. I did not know what I would be doing. All I saw was that the average pay for direct care staff was near

$30K a year. That seemed like a lot to me. I applied. Had an interview a few days later. Went to it and hoped. The job seemed exciting to me. I liked the idea of working a block shift: go to work on one day, stay a few nights, then go home and have all that time off. I waited for a week, or perhaps it was two weeks, to receive a call for an offer. The person who interviewed me said he would call. I'm sure almost all job interviewers say that, but experience has shown me that this is often a lie.

My mom and I went to visit Bub in Connecticut. We arrived on a Friday morning after driving all night. I received a call while I was sleeping that they were offering me a job. I later discovered that the person who interviewed me was not authorized to offer me a position. But the joke is now on the director who reprimanded him, because I have been with the company ever since. It is the only full-time job I've ever had.

I wanted to quit Pyramid right away. Bub, however, said that would be a dangerous precedent for me. Correction: In an extremely gentle way, he told me that quitting becomes a habit that is hard to break. He helped me craft a very professional two-weeks-notice letter, eloquently outlining my reasons for resigning my position, thanking them for the opportunity, and giving the date of my last day. That letter was so good that the director complimented it when she received it. She, of course, attempted to defend herself and her actions, promising me that the next counselor position that opened would be mine. I had heard that before, and I politely declined.

I will talk about one more time when Bub was there for me. I was having what was up to that time one of the darkest times of my life. In 1998 into the fall of 1999, I became the victim of a catfishing scheme. I met a woman named Marianne on a website that was active at the time called Sony Station. On there, you could play Jeopardy! and Wheel of Fortune against real people. You could also start chats and private conversations with people you played the games with. Marianne and I started to chat and get to know each other. I never thought for a second that this person could be lying; I was painfully unaware of my naivety in the ways of the internet. I was a country boy; I didn't know the ways of the world. After we'd been talking for a while into the summer of 1999,

I noticed that many times the things that she promised never came to fruition. I began to think things weren't as they seemed. I demanded that she tell me the truth on the phone one day. When we first started talking, she was twenty-one years old. Then she was twenty-four, then twenty-six. She told me she hadn't wanted to tell me the truth about her age because I was only nineteen and wouldn't want to be with a woman who was so much older than me. That didn't seem to be the truth to me. I demanded a picture of her, and she said she would send some. She never did, at least not pictures of herself. She sent me pictures of someone I didn't know who was in a bikini—a woman who was beautiful with an amazing body. It bought her more time. Then she told me she would send me money to pay my phone bill and to buy stuff I needed to get. The check never showed up. Bub was there for me and gave me the money I needed.

That summer I decided that even though I had already been accepted for the fall semester at Mount Union, I would take a break before starting college. I can't seem to put myself back into the mindset of why I wanted that break, but I am sure Marianne had something to do with it, I wanted to spend more "time" with her, although we only talked on the phone and the internet. Bub was working at a hotel restaurant as a server. He talked to his boss and got me an interview, which was token because I already had the job. He helped me in that way, too, so I could make my own money as a dishwasher. I hated it, but it was money. Eventually, I just got in my car and drove to where Marianne lived. It was a long drive into West Virginia. I found her house eventually and knocked on the door. An obese woman answered the door. When I asked for Marianne, she said Marianne had just left, that she was her friend, and that Marianne had told her she would be gone for a few hours. I said I would wait, and I sat in the driveway for about five hours, and no one ever came. I finally left and went home. A week or two later, I heard from Marianne again for the first time. She was angry that I had just showed up unannounced. I said I wanted the truth. She told me she was the woman who had answered the door when I knocked. I thought she was lying about that. I was stupid; I know that now. I couldn't believe

I would be so stupid as to fall for lies. She then invited me down for a visit. I stupidly went down, and when I spent some time with her and heard her talk, I knew then that it was her. I made the visit and then left. Later she invited me down for Thanksgiving. I stupidly went down again. This time, I vowed to stay. Even though I knew the truth, I thought the only thing she had lied to me about was her appearance and age. She turned out to be thirty-eight years old. Everything else was her and what I had fallen for. I didn't want to be a person who only cared about the packaging of a woman. The rest turned out to be nothing but lies as well. She had a guy living with her. She told me it was her brother. Turned out it was her son.

While I was there, I think she poisoned me. Whether deliberately or not, I don't know. I just know that one night I got very sick. I was sick for the entire weekend. I was sleeping on her floor in a spare room because I refused to sleep in a bed with her.

On Monday, I called my mom and set up a scheme for her to get me out of there because I didn't have the courage to pull myself out of that situation on my own. We worked out that my uncle Cecil had almost ripped his thumb off while putting a tarp on the trailer of his truck, and that he lost a lot of blood, and I was the only one in the family who could give blood to him. The accident was true, but it had happened a few weeks before, and I didn't actually need to donate blood to him. When I got home, my mom and Bub were both there. Bub was the first to hug me as I sobbed into his arms, screaming about how I was "so fucking stupid. Fucking dumb as hell."

Bub said, "You fucked up. Just learn from it. I love you."

He supported me, helped me up physically. We didn't talk about it too much after that. I eventually cut ties with her completely. Even that took some time, even after I returned home.

After that, I was working at Walmart in the seasonal department in layaway. I decided then that the best option for me was to go back to school. My acceptance letter from the summer of 1998 was still valid. I called the admissions office, and they told me I did not need to worry about being accepted, I just need to pay the application fee again. But I didn't have the money for the application fee. I called a few people, and no one could help me. My mom called Bub and asked if he could help me. He called me back ten minutes later and said he would bring me the money the next day. I am not sure if he had the money or if he had to borrow it himself, but he never wanted me to pay him back. Then I opted for Ohio University instead because it was less than half the cost. I hated it, though. Bub had said I would. I ended up going back to Mount Union College. Because of the money Bub gave me, I was able to enroll at Mount Union in the spring semester of 2000.

Now, I don't know if this next story is something Bub did from the grave or not. I think it is worth mentioning, and I'll let everyone decide for themselves. A few years ago, I got to thinking about Marianne again. I was curious about what happened to her. So I got online to see if I could figure out what she was doing with her life. I found out that she had died in a single-car accident on a bitter December night. According to the police report, there were no apparent causes for the accident. There were no skid marks, no evidence of hitting an animal, nothing that showed that anything happened other than she lost control. I felt guilty when I found out about it because I had wished her dead so many times over the years. Plus, when I found out, I still firmly believed that my thoughts could kill someone. A friend of mine pointed out this was a case of the Schrödinger's Cat theory.

CHAPTER 16

Sports

Sports were always a tie that bound my brother and me together. We used to go out in the yard and play pass with a football or a baseball, or we would go play home run derby, one-on-one basketball, two-hand touch football, or hockey. We'd go fishing, and there were probably some games that we made up ourselves. Sports were a constant, whether we watched each other play, watched together, or went out in the yard and played.

Some of my earliest memories are of going to watch his Little League baseball games. My mom would buy me a bag of chips, a Mountain Dew, and either a hot dog or a piece of pizza, and I would quietly sit in the stands and watch the game. Running around and being a wild child was something I never did. I was there to watch the game, and my brother. An outstanding player he was. He could have played at higher levels than Little League. Track, though, became his passion. He was a crazy person who ran the distance races: 800 meters, 1600 meters and 3200 meters. He was good at the 4 by 800-meter relay, too. Almost every track meet he ran, my mom and I attended. Our Aunt Pat would often attend also, bringing her mini camcorder, and our Aunt Eunice. I didn't understand track at all when he first started running. After his first race, he came up to the fence, and I said, "Sorry you didn't win."

He said, "I came in first place."

I asked, "How? There were a bunch of people in front of you."

He said, "I don't race everyone. We all run together, but I'm only racing against whatever school we are going against."

After that, I understood and could keep track of when he would run and know who he was running against. The only time he raced everyone was when there was an invitational.

He also ran cross country in high school. After the three high schools in our school district combined into one high school, the enrollment and interest were sufficient to support a cross-country team. I believe Bub liked cross country more than track. He never stopped running. He ran in many 5Ks and 10Ks and even the New York City marathon. He was still running not long before his death. He was having trouble keeping his feet under him, and he fell, injuring himself on the head in the week before he died.

We went to many Pirates games; some of those adventures I described in other chapters. We also went to Steelers games. I remember going to a game in 2003, the Steelers versus the San Diego Chargers. Bub bought my mom, my Aunt Eunice, and myself tickets to the game as a Christmas present. In that game, Jerome Bettis surpassed Marcus Allen on the all-time rushing list, which was why we went to that particular game. We wanted to see history. We saw it.

Bub used to come to my baseball games sometimes when I played in high school. He thought I had the talent to play in college, perhaps even professionally. I don't know that I was that good, but hearing that from him always made me feel good. No, strike that. I didn't feel good hearing those words; I felt damn near invincible. His praise was something I always wanted and desired. Not that he withheld it often. He always praised me, but I put him on such a pedestal that when he bestowed those words on me, it felt like being knighted by the queen.

Some fun that we always had during football season while watching games on TV at home: During halftime, or before the games started, we would go outside and play one on one with our dad as all-time quarterback. Dad would draw up plays in his hand, and we would run them. Bub always beat me. One thing I can say is that he never took it easy on me just because I was younger. He never thought I would get better that way. One time we were playing in the front yard. I was on offense, and Dad threw me a pass. Bub jumped up and tipped it just before it got to me. Its trajectory changed, and the point hit me right in the eye, giving me a black eye that lasted for about a week after. He thought it was hilarious.

Sports have brought us together as a family even in Bub's death. Ever since he died, if I am not working, I watch almost every Steelers game with my parents—and with my brother. We bring his ashes out and cover his urn with his Myron Cope's Official Terrible Towels. Any time we need a big play to happen, we tap his urn and say, "Come on, Bubba, we need [whatever type of play we need for the offense or defense]!" We do the same thing when we watch the Penguins. Unfortunately, the Pirates haven't been very good for most of my life, and certainly for only a couple years since Bub died, so we don't really watch baseball together.

One Steelers game we watched together will have to stand for all the others. It is the most important story to tell, anyway. It was January 2009, less than a year after Bub's death. The Steelers were playing their bitterest rivals, the Baltimore Ravens. Those games are always hard-hitting, brutal games. In my opinion, it is the best rivalry in all of sport. It was a very close game throughout. The Steelers had a lead late in the game. The Ravens had the ball, and they could drive down the field and take the lead. They had a rookie quarterback named Joe Flacco who had been a thorn in the side of the Steelers. Would this be the drive with the biggest thorn of them all? Would Flacco start his career off by taking the Ravens to the Super Bowl?

Bub's favorite player was Troy Polamalu. We think it was because Troy had long flowing hair and played the game with reckless abandon. He was the type of player Bub just absolutely loved: the ones who played the game fast and out of control but were actually extremely cerebral players. Polamalu was the player for whom we most frequently asked Bubba for big plays.

Baltimore drove down the field. Then Troy struck. He picked off his pass from a position that, he said in an interview later, he wasn't supposed to be in. The defensive play called for him to be somewhere else, but he was so smart, he read the situation and knew where he needed to be. He took the chance. He made the play, and then, to quote Mike Tomlin, he "did what Troy does, he cut back." He cut back, all right. He went all the way to end zone, clinching the AFC Championship for the Steelers.

The story of this game doesn't end there, however. If you go back and watch that play, if you pay close attention when Troy goes into the end zone, there is a yellow terrible towel lying in the white section of the back of the end zone. Our family has always steadfastly believed that that was my brother's terrible towel. We say this because after that night, his yellow terrible towel disappeared and has never been seen again. We think he dropped it there to tell us he is doing fine in heaven. Thank you to our cousin Jay for spotting that terrible towel. I can't watch that game without weeping at the end.

The Steelers went to defeat the Arizona Cardinals in the Super Bowl. It was a great game with a historic play of its own, a drive by James Harrison. And it had a great catch to clinch the win by one of Bub's Ohio State guys, Santonio Holmes. When LaMarr Woodley sacked Kurt Warner to clinch the game, I stripped down to my boxers, sprinted out the front door, ran barefoot through the snow, and dove onto our concrete memorial for Bub. Hugging it and crying, I screamed, "We did it, Bub! WE DID IT!"

Bub continued to bring us championships in 2009. Our beloved Penguins were in the Stanley Cup Finals. For the second straight year, they were playing the perennial powerhouse Detroit Red Wings, or, as I like to call them, the Detroit Bleeding Pussies. The Penguins had lost in six games in the 2007–'08 season, and it looked like they were going to lose in six games again. They were down 3–2 in the series. They pulled game six out, though, by a score of 2–1. Then it was on to Joe Louis Arena for game seven. I decided at the last minute to go to Jay's house to watch the game. We got wings to eat, symbolizing our desire to crush the Wings. The Penguins got off to a great start, thanks to the unlikeliest of guys: Maxine Talbot, who had gotten his face beaten in during the Philadelphia series in order to change the momentum because the Penguins were down 3–0 and in danger of losing control of the series. After that fight, which he lost, he shushed the crowd by putting his finger to his lips. In game seven, he quieted the Detroit crowd quickly by scoring a mere 1:13 into the game. He scored again about nine minutes later. That was all the goals the Penguins would score in the entire game, but, luckily, it would be just enough. Detroit scored in the third period, making the final six minutes of the game an exercise in nerves and anxiety. I swear, no clock has ever ticked down slower in my life. In the waning seconds of the game, Detroit had an open net, and one of their best players had the puck on his stick. He shot toward the net. Jay and I were jumping up and down at this point, yelling various words, making noises, and cussing like sailors. Then, flying across the goal's yawning net was number 29 of the Pittsburgh Penguins, goalie Marc-André Fleury.

(This is the same Marc-André Fleury who had struggled during his rookie season. Our mom said, "This guy isn't very good." Jay responded, "He's going to be great." By game seven of that Stanley Cup Final, Fleury had become our mom's favorite player. That she found him attractive may or may not have been a factor in this.)

The puck hit Fleury squarely on the chest and bounced away, and time ran out. We were the Stanley Cup Champions! Jay and I were dancing and jumping and hugging and crying and saying, "Thank you, Bub!" over and over again.

The Penguins have won two more cups since 2009, and those wins were very satisfactory, but that first one in 2009 will forever be special, especially coming as it did on the heels of the Steelers' Super Bowl win. Those will forever be Bub's championships. Those wins helped, maybe only minutely, to bind some of the open wound that has been ever-present in me since the day Bub died.

CHAPTER 17

Videogames

Grief is a funny thing. And I certainly don't mean the ha-ha kind of funny, that's for goddamn sure. So many strange things go through a person's mind in times of grief—other than the obvious denial of the truth, I mean. The cycling through the stages of grief can be so rapid. It's almost like they step on one another as they vie to take over the conscious mind. One of the first thoughts I had after initially settling down from hearing of my brother's death was, "I guess I will save money at Christmastime since I won't need to buy him a present." I had that thought repeatedly, and I do not know why it was there. I never struggled to buy gifts for my family. At that time, my wife and I even picked names off the giving tree at the library. I always struggled to decide what to get Bub, but it wasn't because of money, that is for sure. He had a good job and never wanted much. If he wanted it, he bought it himself. So he was hard to buy for. I always figured something out, though. So I don't know what that thought about saving money was for. It fucking sucks to remember it. I feel selfish, self-centered, ugly, and like I didn't deserve to be the one left alive.

Other weird aspects of grief are the way it surprises you. Right after the start of the grief, or years later, any time of day or night, grief has the power to surprise you. It pops up around corners and make you think about things. I remember going through my mundane everyday activities in the days, weeks and months after his death, and the thought would pop into my head, "Bub will never do this again." I'd go to McDonald's and think, "Bub will never call me to get Minnie fries from AJ and Marty again." Going to Ponderosa, I'd think: "Bub will never eat at a buffet again." Listening to a new song: "Bub will never hear this song."

It is hard to go through experiences that I know he either loved or would have loved. I mentioned the example of Star Wars earlier. It's hard knowing that Bub will never get to see the newer movies in that franchise.

Thinking about this, I am reminded of when Bub was determined to get an original Nintendo. He mowed grass, worked with our dad on the Dyes' farm, and saved and saved to get it. He was so excited to get it. Honestly, so was I. It was the start of my video game addiction, which continues to this day.

Before the Nintendo, though, Uncle Jack gave Bub a Commodore 64. He loved that thing. I still don't understand how it worked. Bub, though, would sit there and meticulously put in the code, I guess it was called, and then we could play games, do our homework, and just have general fun with it. He could use cartridge games with it, too. He had three different games, but the only one I really remember playing is the baseball game. That was so much fun. Something I remember about it: Bub never complained that I wanted to play. He shared his computer with me. He even tried to teach me how to input the code. I never grasped it. I just let him do that, and I reaped the rewards of his hard work.

Before the Nintendo, we had an Atari, and I remember watching our mom and Bub play some games on that. But I don't remember playing it all that much. Some *River Raid* is about all I remember playing on that system. Like I said, Nintendo started my addiction. I would sit at school and think about playing when I got home.

Back to the Nintendo: It was Bub's; he worked and paid for it. He could have easily, and probably rightly, denied me access to it at any time. He never did, though. He got two controllers so we could play together. We played the greats: *Duck Hunt, Mario Bros. 1* and *2, Legend of Zelda, Tecmo Bowl, Tecmo Super Bowl, Ice Hockey,* and two of our favorites that took most of our time and effort: *All-Star Baseball* and *Metal Gear.* We even got our dad to play *Tecmo Super Bowl.* He may or may not have gotten so pissed at the game that he broke a controller or two.

Metal Gear was our favorite, though. Bub had a notebook full of the codes that the game gave you when you saved so you could pick up where you left off. We had never seen a game like it before. It was amazing. It captivated us: the story, the idea of the game itself. We both put a lot of time into that game. Funnily enough, we never beat that game because it wasn't a straightforward game. It wasn't linear; we didn't understand that until long after we played it out. You had to get in a truck and travel back and forth several times to get to the final board and enter a building and get to the end, which was timed. It seemed, and still seems to this day, impossible. We still loved it even though it was super frustrating. Sometimes that makes a game fun.

As Bub got older and did more stuff outside the house, I got new game systems and played games by myself. But there was one significant exception. In 1998, I got a PlayStation 1. For that system, there was another Metal Gear game released. It was called *Metal Gear Solid: Tactical Espionage Action*. I didn't get the game until 1999, in the spring. Bub would come home from his apartment, and we would stay up all night playing it. I had played it before while in college. During my first round of midterms at Ohio University, my neighbors and I rented the game, and we all took turns playing it. Again, none of us had ever played a game like that. The game was smart. It interacted with your system. You had to be smart to play it. You had to think your way through it; you couldn't just barrel through every section and beat it. That would lead to dying again and again. I knew the trick, but I wanted to see if my brother could figure it out. Took him about two minutes. Dude was so fucking smart.

Fast-forwarding a few years, after he was living in Connecticut, he got his own PlayStation 1. He would bring it home and play his World War 2 games. This was the time I mentioned earlier when he would bring out Mickey, his cockatiel, and ask him, "Hey Mick, want to kill kraut?"

Mick was always willing and learned to say "Kill Kraut" ever after.

When I was home, we would still have Metal Gear marathons. In 2001, *Metal Gear Solid 2: Sons of Liberty* was released. I remember when we played the game for the first time. He'd had it for a week, but he waited to open it up and play it until he came home. He had a PlayStation 2 at this time; I still had a PS1. I felt honored that he wanted to wait, knowing how excited he was to play the game. We started playing as Snake, but then Snake appears to die at the end of the prologue and you have to switch to playing as Raiden. I remember we were sad because we wanted to be Snake. Eventually, though, we learned to love that game. Then, in 2004, perhaps the greatest video game ever created was released, *Metal Gear 3: Snake Eater.* Again, nothing like that game had ever existed before. It blew our fucking minds. We played it through in one weekend during Christmas, then started playing it all over again. We beat it twice within a week and never stopped loving it.

In 2008, Konami was going to release a new Metal Gear game. This was for the PlayStation 3, which had just been released. At Christmas of 2007, when Bub came home, he talked about how excited he was to play it. He was going to trade in his PlayStation 2 and get a PS3 just so he could play it. His excitement was palpable. I was excited too, for him and myself. I was upset, though, when I learned it would only be released for the PS3. I had an Xbox at the time. Bub never got to play that game. It came out in June 2008. I decided when it came out to trade my Xbox in toward a PS3. They were releasing a bundle with the new Metal Gear game, *Metal Gear Solid 4: Guns of the Patriots.* The console had a gunmetal gray case. That system looked so sweet. The day I brought it home, Audrey was working and I was home alone with our cats. My baby Stormy, sensing that I was sad, as he so often could do, crawled into my lap. I cried and fired up the system and started to play *Guns of the Patriots.* I cried almost the entire time that first day. It was and is a great game. Sadly, I can't play it these days. Because of some weird thing with the coding for the PS3, the games don't translate to the newer generations of PlayStation.

The next game, released for the PS4, was *Metal Gear Solid V: Ground Zeroes,* followed by *Metal Gear Solid V: The Phantom Pain.* It was a two-part game, with *Ground Zeroes* being a sort of prologue to the other one. *The Phantom Pain* is the most comprehensive game of the series I have played. It is an open world game. The story is extremely deep and involved. It is a great game, and seemingly endless. I currently have a save going on with it right now. I have logged over 125 hours of game-play and still don't have it at 100% completed. Probably never will.

Last year, though, 2023, Konami remastered the first three games: *Solid Snake* from 1998, *Sons of Liberty* from 2001, and *Snake Eater* from

2004. I was so very excited for this to happen, especially since the release date was close to my birthday. So I took that week off from work. I then went to my parents' house and got my brother's ashes, and for the next week did nothing but play Metal Gear. I complained to my mom that Bub wouldn't take his turn, "because he doesn't have thumbs." She said, "He's all right, just play the game." It was bittersweet to play with him there with me yet unable to play.

As I sit here today in June 2024, I am harboring a ton of excitement once again for Metal Gear. They are not just remastering *Snake Eater*, they are remaking it under the name of *Metal Gear Delta*. There is no official release date, but you can rest assured that when it comes out, Bub and I will be sitting side by side playing once again.

CHAPTER 18

Everybody Hurts: Others' Stories

I mentioned earlier that I would be including some perspectives on my brother's life from people outside of the immediate family so everyone can get a more well-rounded picture of just how amazing Bub was. Some of these stories are about his living life, when he was still with us. Others are about how he's helped us out in life as our angel.

Stories from Our Cousin Lisa McCourt

The first story is from our cousin Lisa. Lisa was born the same year as Bub, about six weeks before him. She posted the following story on Facebook. Here it is verbatim.

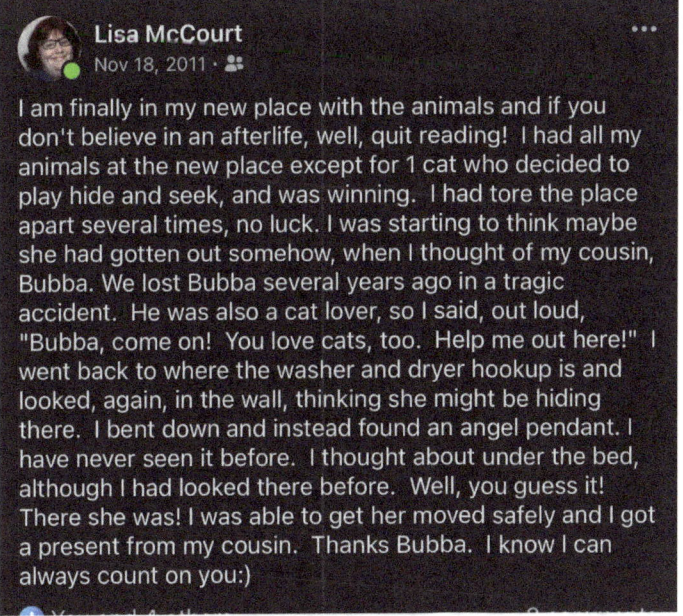

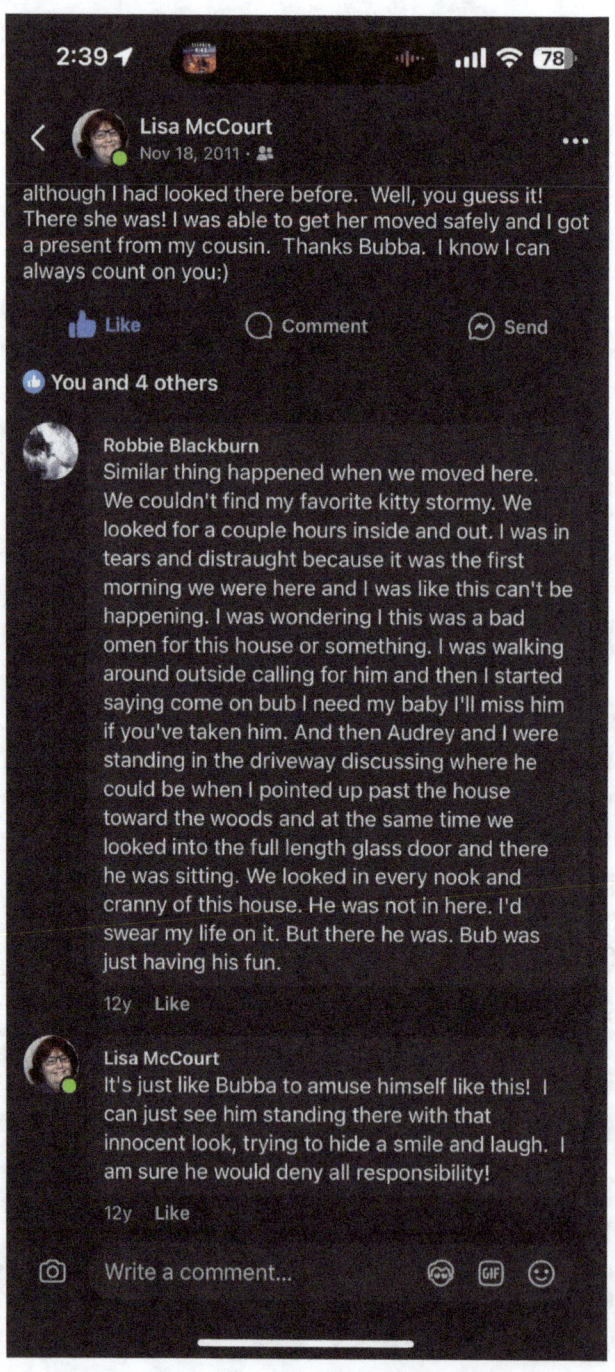

Lisa McCourt
Nov 18, 2011

although I had looked there before. Well, you guess it! There she was! I was able to get her moved safely and I got a present from my cousin. Thanks Bubba. I know I can always count on you:)

👍 Like   💬 Comment   📨 Send

👍 You and 4 others

Robbie Blackburn
Similar thing happened when we moved here. We couldn't find my favorite kitty stormy. We looked for a couple hours inside and out. I was in tears and distraught because it was the first morning we were here and I was like this can't be happening. I was wondering I this was a bad omen for this house or something. I was walking around outside calling for him and then I started saying come on bub I need my baby I'll miss him if you've taken him. And then Audrey and I were standing in the driveway discussing where he could be when I pointed up past the house toward the woods and at the same time we looked into the full length glass door and there he was sitting. We looked in every nook and cranny of this house. He was not in here. I'd swear my life on it. But there he was. Bub was just having his fun.

12y   Like

Lisa McCourt
It's just like Bubba to amuse himself like this! I can just see him standing there with that innocent look, trying to hide a smile and laugh. I am sure he would deny all responsibility!

12y   Like

Write a comment...

Bub gets his fair share of blame for things that go wrong, especially anything electrical. One day, I complained about my brother's cat AJ when I was at my parents' house, the next day my PlayStation stopped working. It was too much of a coincidence to be a coincidence. Bella, one of my male cats, the day I was rooting against Ohio State, Bub's favorite college team, walked right over in front of me and urinated into my outlet. This was easy to do, my house is very old, and the outlets are on the floor. I just felt like Bub had persuaded Bella to do it for rooting again his team. Anything that happens, we blame him because he would enjoy our problems and sit back and laugh, as Lisa says above and below.

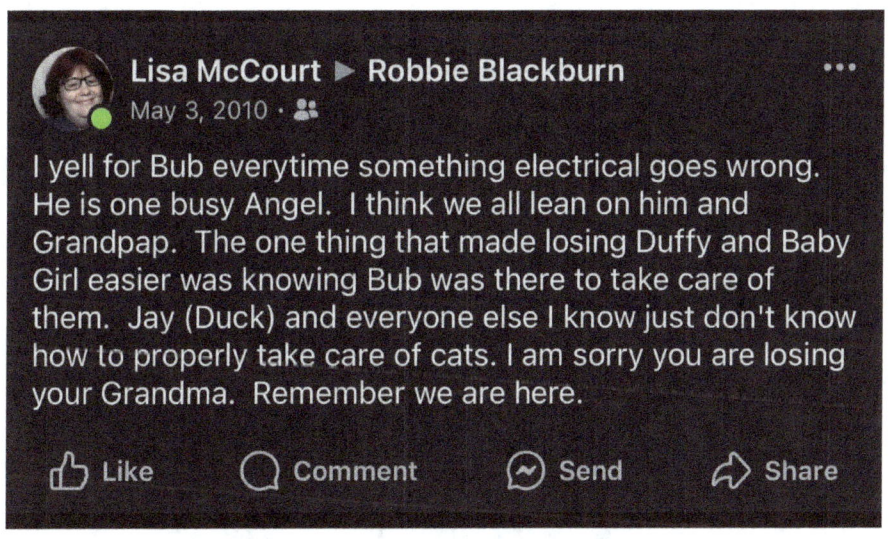

Story from Mike Loftus

If I had to name my brother's best friend in high school, the person he hung out with the most, the person he talked about the most when he was at home, it would undoubtedly be Mike Loftus. Mike was a year behind Bub in school, but they still ran track and cross country together. After Mike graduated, he went on to serve in the Air Force. Thank you for your service, Mike. I remember when I made the decision to send out messages to Bub's friends from his teenage years to let them know

117

he had died. The message to Mike was one of the hardest ones to send, because I knew he was on deployment and I knew just how close they were. They kept in touch through MySpace. Mike told me that when he was finished with his deployment, they were going to hang out in Wisconsin. I felt terrible because I knew Mike wouldn't be able to come back to Ohio and be there for a funeral.

I posted on Facebook several years ago, asking people to tell me humorous stories about Bub. It was an effort to counter the nightmares I described previously. Below is one story that Mike posted and our back and forth about it.

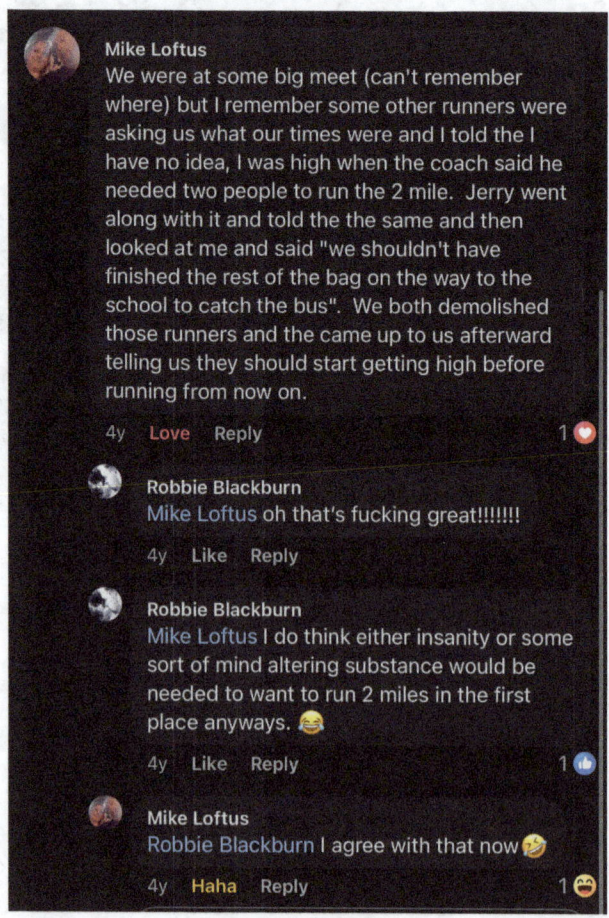

Story from Uncle Jack via Mom

This is a story I heard secondhand that I am going to relay here. My mom told it to me. First, a little background.

If we were to name who amongst our aunts and uncles favored Bub most of all, it would be Uncle Jack. Before I was thought of and soon after I was born, Bub always stayed with Uncle Jack as often as he could get permission. As you may remember, it was Uncle Jack who brought him to meet me for the first time. They did a lot of things together. The stories that most frequently were told were about the two of them staying up to watch Johnny Carson on *The Tonight Show*. They also always watched sports together, mostly baseball and football. Uncle Jack liked to teach Bub fun swears to yell at the players.

Mentioning that Bub was Uncle Jack's favorite nephew leads to the story I mentioned before, the one my mom told me. The day Bub died, Uncle Jack's first grandchild was born. The first time he saw my mom after he found out, he gave her a tight hug, crying his eyes out, and sobbed into her ear: "I feel like I traded your son for my granddaughter. I am so sorry. I would never have done that. I love him so much."

Stories from My Cousin Jay

Jay sent me the following stories.

Bub and I shared more than a first name. We are both named Jerry. We both have always been called by names by the family other than our first names. I'm called Jay, my middle name. I don't blame Bub for not wanting to be called his middle name, Eugene. Bub and I shared a bond unlike I have with many of our other cousins. We are both the older siblings and our younger siblings were always brats. So we bonded over that. We spent the most time together as we were growing up. Robb and Lisa (my sister) hung out with each other, as brats will do. I have many stories of us growing up together.

My favorite story though happened when we were going to see Slayer in concert. It was me, him, and our cousin Tommy, which we sometimes call Pete. I don't know why, we just do. I was driving, Bub was in the passenger seat and Tommy in the back. We were driving across the Market Street Bridge in Steubenville, Ohio. I was stopped at the red-light, which has always been a long ass light. Bub, who had spotted a can of spray paint in the trunk, told me to pop the hatch. I did, and he jumped out, grabbed the can of paint and painted on the guardrail of the bridge the slay logo. I was shocked. This seemed so out of character for him. Robb has the picture, I'll tell him to put it in below.

Graffiti by Bub.

This wasn't the end of the day's surprises from him. This was in the early 90s before interstate 22 was completed to bypass Weirton, West Virginia. we had to drive through downtown. As I was driving, Bub leans out the window and screams at this old lady carrying two brown paper bags of groceries, "SLAYER FUCKING SLAYER". She screamed and swung her arms up and her groceries went everywhere. I have been to too many concerts in my life. This memory is always one that is within easy reach.

* * *

Robb still doesn't believe me, but I have the scar on my eyebrow to prove it. A scar that Bub caused. Our uncle Fred had just moved down by the creek. There was this building there we were cleaning out. Bub picked up this old thermos. The red checked one. I think they are made of steel. For some reason, he just whipped it at me hard. So hard that when it hit me, the glass on the inside broke. Hurt like a bitch, and I have that scar as a reminder.

* * *

We used to go camping on my Dad's property, sometimes it was my Granny's. We would get alcohol from someone, usually my cousin Steph, who was older than me. We'd all drink the bottle, sharing it back and forth. Bub and I were almost always there. Sometimes Freddie would join us, Robb, Ivan, Dink and I think even a couple times Tommy joined us before he got to where he refused to leave the house. These camping trips were always a blast. Sometimes we used a tent, sometimes we just slept under the stars. A few times I had found this flat spot on near these cliffs. These cliffs have their own funny story. Bub and Robb were walking over the hill to the spot. It was a big hill, probably a mile walk. Bub and Robb almost walked right off the cliff and into a mine pond. We also used to find old truck tires randomly on the hill and then roll them down the hill. They also made an excellent fuel for our campfires.

Something else that was funny, but made me a little mad. Bub was driving my four wheeler. He was determined to get through this mud hole. He didn't make it. We had to get my dad to pull it out of the mud. It was buried beyond the back tires and wouldn't move at all.

Story from Dan

My friend Dan offers this story.

Robb worked on a cruise ship in 2003. When he was finished with his hitch, Mom, I call their Mom my Mom as well, and I went to pick him up. There was a blackout up that way. Bub said we didn't have to come and that he would bring Robb back home. Mom said we are coming, anyway. What I remember most was that we drove down to Stamford, Connecticut, from New London where Bub lived. We caught the subway. I'm using that because I know Robb hates that T word, and took it into New York City at Grand Central. Bub who was used to running and walking everywhere walked us all over New York. The next day, my legs were so sore I could barely move. When I complained about the pain Bub said "You pussy, that wasn't anything." And laughed at me. Another fun memory from that trip was on the trip home. There was a car that had a Jesus themed bumper sticker and cut us off on the highway. Robb blurted out, "Jesus wants you to use turn signals!"

That trip will always be one of my favorites. Not only because we brought my little brother home, that I hadn't seen in months, but because I got shown New York as well. Bub was always up for an adventure. Bub always treated me like family. I never felt like he didn't love me as much as Robb. He would pick on me, tease me and do all the things an older brother is supposed to do.

When Tiffany called and told that Robb had called her, I was in complete shock. I remember going over to Mom and Dad's and just being there. I remember standing on the porch holding her up. Some people suggested giving her something for shock to calm her down. I said, "Mom, No one is giving you anything on my watch while I'm here."

I barely left their house over the next week or two. Robb and I played NHL Hockey on his Xbox damn near nonstop. We celebrated the Penguins trading for a guy from the Atlanta Thrashers, then we mourned the loss of another icon in our lives as Pittsburgh Steelers fans the same week, Myron Cope.

Stories involving Aunt Ellen

Aunt Ellen is our dad's older sister. She was always the fun Blackburn to be around because she did so many interesting things, especially to two kids who were in awe of her anyway. I have a very distinct memory of being at her house in Salem, Ohio, and I know the date precisely because it was a historic event, not only for the sporting world but also for the Blackburn brothers. The date was November 22, 1986, and the event was Mike Tyson's first title fight against Trevor Berbick. The event that happened for us that made our history, and thus our story, was that this was the first time my brother and I ever had pizza delivered. We avoided the Noid and got Domino's. I was awestruck, as a seven-year-old, that you could have food, especially my favorite food, delivered at any time. I always dreamed of living in a place where I could have this done because growing up in a very rural place, food delivery was a pipe dream. The fight was memorable, if very short. Tyson won in the second round by a technical knockout. He became the youngest champion in boxing history.

Aunt Ellen was always fascinating. She played softball as an adult on an organized team. She traveled all over the place and competed. As I remember, she was very good. Perhaps I got my baseball prowess from her; I was always considered a pretty excellent player. Another sport she took part in was something I had only seen on TV until that time. She was a roller derby Doll. I couldn't even skate, and she was not only skating but fighting with other women at the same time. It was mesmerizing to watch her skill and strength, even though I am not sure I ever really understood what was going on.

One of the better things about Aunt Ellen was that she never seemed to treat us as afterthoughts just because we were kids. I remember one time, when I was probably six and Bub ten, we went to her house for family poker night. We were invited to play with her, our dad, and our great-grandpap Jake Board (who I got my middle name from). Grandpap Board was a character. He loved to play poker, but only one game: five-card stud. He said it was the only true poker game. He abhorred games that had wild cards; he would sit those games out, grumbling the entire time that they were bullshit while sipping his Pabst Blue Ribbon beer. One time I accidentally picked it up and took a drink. That shit was nasty. Bub's game of choice was Follow the Queen, a game where you got two cards down to start as hole cards, then everyone got one card up. If a queen showed up, the next card was considered a wild card. If no queen showed, only queens were wild, and if more than one queen showed, the next card following the last queen was wild. It was a game of unpredictability in a game already fraught with unpredictability.

Something else Aunt Ellen provided us with was the ability to meet animals we probably would have never encountered otherwise. She raised llamas. We would go to her house, and then she would take us to the llama farm to help her feed them and groom them. Fascinating animals. They never seemed to like me. They would always try to bite me or, more frequently, spit on me. But Bub? They loved him.

Story from my friend Jackie

There are countless memories I could share about Jerry, but the ones that stand out most to me are from our time in cross country. Despite Jerry being on the high school team and me just a middle school newbie, he never made me feel like a "kid" in comparison. One especially special memory that comes to mind is a classic high school goof-up that I still laugh about today.

Our practice runs always took us to the lake, which was a bit of a distance from the school. Those high schoolers lucky enough to have cars would give us rides there. One day, early in my running journey, some of the older students thought it would be hilarious to lock me in the trunk of Jerry's car. Jerry, known for his spirited driving and taking corners like a race car driver, unknowingly drove me through those winding country roads to the park.

Feeling every bump and twist along the way, I'm still not sure if Jerry realized I was in the trunk, but he was the one who eventually let me out. Looking back, it was just kids being kids, and a story I fondly reminisce about. Despite the prank, it felt like Jerry had my back from that day forward . . . and without him, I never would have met his brother, one of my closest friends.

CHAPTER 19

How and Why I Write

Bub always told me I was very creative. He said my poetry proved that to him. I don't know how creative I am. I just come up with stuff, and sometimes I write it down. Sometimes I keep myself awake at night, long after I should have gone to sleep, creating scenarios for all aspects of life, whether it is a grand scheme to get myself out of debt, playing out a poker tournament that I'm planning to play in soon, or some confrontation that is upcoming, such as with a client's shitty psychiatrist. I lie there and create all these scenarios, complete with dialogue and all. I even rewrite the scenario in multiple ways, attempting to map out all the ways a conversation might go. Rarely does my imagination nail what happens in reality. But I always do this. I can't help but do it. I've always entertained myself by telling myself stories.

I guess now I've written some of them down. Three of them so far, with starts and notes for three other books, along with this one. Not that this is taking much of my creative mind to come up with. This has just flowed like a stream in the woods—nice and cool, calm and collected. Nothing I've written has been a struggle to write once I started. There haven't been starts and fits. Once I sit down and type, it just comes. I'm doing other things at the same time. For example, at this moment, I'm listening to an audiobook on the lead-up to the Civil War and playing PlayStation online with my friend, all while I write. While writing other chapters of this book, I have listened to audiobooks from the *Dark Tower* series and the *Harry Potter* series, one about Grant in Vicksburg, and one on Gettysburg. Sometimes I'm doing all three things at once. My brain often must have multiple activities going on, or I can't concentrate. There is probably a diagnosis for this, but I don't want it any other way.

Going back to when I first lived with Dan in 2003 and '04, I've always had two TVs: one to play video games on and one to watch. I can keep up with both things, whatever I'm playing and watching.

While I'm doing all that, my brain comes up with some things that even I find somewhat impressive. One of those things was a poem I wrote several years ago. I'm adding it here because my brother's influence is there, dripping from every line. This is because of his love for music. He favored heavy metal, but he was fine with listening to anything. So, as his little brother, I too listened to everything. None of the lines of this next poem are my own words. All the lines of this poem are song lyrics or song titles I put together to create a poem. Ultimately they seem to go together and create a coherent piece with a clear meaning, at least to me. With that being said, here is a testament to my brother's influence and the creativity he said I possess:

SONGS WE KNOW, DEPTH WE WERE UNSURE

You got to fight for your right
Tonight tonight
Otherwise it'll be
Good riddance, the time of your life
And when I'm gone
I'll just say
Bye bye bye
There'll be no
Tears in heaven
As long as you
Don't stop believin
And you don't let
Cold November rain
Steal your
Minutes to memories
It'll be rain on the scarecrow
Washing away the pain,

That will leave you

Insane in the brain

Leave you feeling

Estranged

There will be no more

Bittersweet me

Just a hope for

Time stand still

Where you can

Dream on

Hoping everything won't be

Gone

And eventually everything will

Carry on

But just maybe

In the end

It'll just be

The end of the world as we know it

And life will have flashed by

In a New York minute

We will have

No excuses

Except this, life was too

Hard to handle

But maybe I can

Hold on

To the right stuff

When all my life

It was

Because the night

And if I fell

You saved my life tonight

When I was

Right next door to hell.

I've always liked this poem. I just wrote it one day in about fifteen minutes, just grabbing pieces of those songs out of thin air and putting them down. It wasn't until after I went back and read the finished poem that I realized it actually conveys a coherent message. Some may see it, some may not. Some may see a completely different message than I do. It is much like I used to tell a friend from college who, when she read my writing, would always ask, "What does it mean?" I would always respond with, "Would you go to a restaurant and ask the chef how something is supposed to taste? No. I can't tell you what it means to you. I know what it means to me. For you, something completely different may be seen. It is up to you to decide what it means."

In all my writing—past, present, and future—I am making my brother proud. I hope the talent he always saw in me will come to fruition and that the stories I may have been born to tell will make it to the world. I feel he would say that they are good enough, although, Even if everything was different from how it is now, if it meant I still had Bub, I would much rather not be writing this memoir. It is helpful, hurtful, cathartic—I've cried as I've written it, I've laughed as I've written. I've had conversations with friends and family, talking about Bub, keeping him alive. Breathing life into a memory until it can almost stand on its own two feet, extend its arms, and give us one more hug to get us through another day of our grieving.

CHAPTER 20

Music, TV, and Books

Younger siblings mimic their older siblings. That's a well-known fact established in the universe. I am no different. For example, my brother grew his hair long. I am now growing my hair long. Some of this is because my wife loves my curls, but I won't lie: Bub's hair influences the decision as well. Another example is my wristbands. When my brother was in eleventh grade, he ran track with a string tied around his wrist. I never knew the purpose of it, but I then tied a string around my wrist. To this day I still wear wristbands. I have ever since I was in sixth grade when I tied that first string around my wrist.

Another way that he still influences me to this day, affecting my life tremendously, is my taste in music. I grew up with him listening to hair metal bands, glam rock, metal, heavy metal, classic rock, and just about everything in between.

I remember one year for Christmas he gave me his Guns N' Roses *Use Your Illusion I* and *II* cassette tapes because he had gotten the CDs and was tired of me borrowing them.

Another major influence he had on me was getting me into Eminem. I had not heard of him, but Bub said that some of the stuff he wrote reminded him of me: some of the cutting lyrics and easy rhymes, along with a natural rhythm that reminded him of my poetry. I have listened to a ton of Eminem in my life now, thanks to Bub. Some of his rhymes and lyrics have even inspired some things that I have written. So, after all this time, my brother influences me in small, subtle, yet significant ways.

Something else he introduced me to was *South Park*. We didn't have Comedy Central on our cable at my parents' house. Bub had moved out and was living in an apartment (oddly enough, it is only about a mile or so from the house of the client I have taken care of for twenty years). I went to Bub's apartment to stay one weekend. We ordered from a pizza outlet that is now called Vocelli's. I had seen the commercials and wanted to try it so badly. It looked delicious, and it was. The pepperoni slices curled up when baked, making them crispy and delicious. I can still almost taste them to this day. Bub then said he wanted me to watch something.

I said, "What?"

He said, "It's called *South Park*. There is a character on there that reminds me of you."

"How?" I asked.

"He's foul-mouthed and will say just about anything to anyone."

Bub then turned on Comedy Central, and I saw my first episode of *South Park*. It was the newest one, called "Chickenlover." It is the one where Cartman is pretending to be a cop and pulls people over on his Big Wheel trike. I was instantly hooked. It was one of the funniest things I ever saw in my life. Within a year I had Cartman plush dolls all over my bed, including the one of him dressed as a cop. "YOU WILL RESPECT MY AUTHORITAH!"

WASTELAND

The featureless face of the demon

No sounds, only noiseless screaming

Painful tears on my cheek

Blazing paths of acidic streak

The world, now just an embodiment of time

Drink up, your thirst craves the blood-filled wine

Hope is lost in the darkest chasm

All I hear is laughter of brethren's sarcasm

All of time, another man's wasteland

The world moves on only for those who understand

The rest of us left behind choking on ill-repute

Comic relief as a deaf mute

Each day grows harder to bear

The doubling of my mind makes me unaware

Two places, two memory sets
I'm caught in a world of someone else's regrets
Two worlds whirling into oblivion
Can't figure out which is a dream
And which I have been living in
I scream out for help
And I'm burned by the sun and touched by the light
    of the moon
All together in one
Here, lost in another world,
Alone at the way-station
My heartbeat, my age hastened
Old before my time
Drink up, your thirst craves the blood-filled wine.

I wrote this poem in late 2003 when I was off from my job working at a facility called Pyramid Healthcare, where I worked with troubled adolescent boys. I hated the job, the hours, and how they screwed me over for a promotion that I was promised, and I hated the drive. It was over an hour each way. The only positive outcome from that job was that one of the boys was reading the first book of the *Dark Tower* Series. I had read a lot of Stephen King in my life at that point, but not for years. College classes cut heavily into reading for pleasure. He lent me *The Gunslinger*. It was very dry, very difficult to read, especially for someone out of practice, but I loved it despite what many call its flaws.

I remember this clearly: I was sitting in my mom's computer room at her desk. I had just finished the third book in the *Dark Tower* series earlier that day, entitled *The Waste Lands*. Snow was coming down heavy outside. I was sitting there wanting to write something that wasn't straightforward—something that could be seen as very deep, layered, and outside the box from my normal writing. I wrote the poem above. I then sent it to my brother. His response was, "That is pretty fucking awesome. It feels like a Testament song. Guess listening to my music in the car fucked your head up."

CHAPTER 21

Guardian Angel

Now, I'm on the fence about some things about this natural world we live in. I can't say for certain the government isn't trying to get us. I don't know if professional sports are scripted, and I don't know if this world is real or a simulation. I'll probably never satisfactorily know the answers to these things. One thing I most assuredly believe in, though, is that we have guardian angels. Bub is mine. It makes sense. He has always been my protector. Also, our guardian angels take requests for help with our loved ones' troubles.

I have two examples of him helping me. One is fresh, like the smoke is still rising from the tires. I am currently at work while I write this. I am sitting in my vehicle watching first responders take care of people who were just involved in a car accident at an intersection. My client and I had just been walking through this same intersection about a minute before the accident. It is very possible we could have and should have been in the intersection at that moment. As we were walking, I had picked out a landmark where we would turn around. But for some reason, when there was still another fifty or sixty feet to go, something compelled me to turn around where we were, which put us through that intersection a minute sooner than we would have been if I had gone with my original plan.

The other example of Bub helping me happened several years ago. I was on my way to work. When I am on my way to work, I always stop at a convenience store and gas station named Sheetz. I went in, got my hot dogs and diet Mountain Dew, and went back to my car. I sat down in my car, and a powerful urge to urinate struck me. I knew I didn't have to go because I had gone not twenty minutes before, when I left the house. I heeded the bladder and went back in to go to the restroom. I get to the urinal, I can't squeeze a drop, as Red from *The Shawshank Redemption* says. I shrug it off and then get in my car to head toward work. I was probably a minute, maybe only forty-five seconds, going back in and then back to my car. I resumed my drive to work, and about ten miles up the highway on a nice bright, sunny December day, no snow, no foul weather at all, there was a three-car wreck. It had to have happened forty-five seconds to a minute before I got there. The wheels of an overturned car were still spinning, smoke was rolling from engines and tires, steam was spewing from busted radiators, and no one had even gotten out of their cars yet. Like I said. Guardian angel.

He works in other ways as well. I'll add two quick notes about asking him to help my new wife and her sister with two different situations.

My wife works at a hospital, and there was this one guy who was creepy as hell who kept stopping in to talk to her, ask her questions, going out of his way to interact with her. She said it made her uncomfortable. I told her I would go talk to the guy if she wanted, but she didn't want a confrontation. So I asked my brother to scare him off. Since I did that, she has only seen the creepy guy on rare occasions, and when she does, he avoids her.

Her sister's situation was similar. Someone she worked with was making her uncomfortable. I asked my brother to intervene. After that, Amanda's sister said that now when she interacted with the guy, he seemed scared of her.

Amanda likes to think of this kind of phenomenon as "woo-woo" bullshit, but we both agree there's some sort of divine intervention going on as well. Sorry, Mrs. McDermott—or Momma Mott, as I affectionately call Amanda's mom—gotta woo here. She hates woos.

CHAPTER 22

Collecting

One of my brother's passions was what he called his "retirement plan." He would spend hours organizing, cataloging, and researching his vast collection of baseball cards. He had thousands. To this day, we still have them stored in large totes, most likely still in the same order and shape they were on the day he died. He always loved them.

I remember as a kid, he would sit in his room with cards spread everywhere, a book or magazine next to him, and a notebook in hand. He meticulously recorded the cards' details, dates, and values, and he tracked the trends. As a future engineer, he liked order and precision. Among his prized possessions were Wade Boggs' cards from every year he played, including his rookie year; Rod Woodson's rookie card; Barry Bonds' rookie card; Mike Gartner's card (he loved this Capitols player); and many more greats from the '80s and '90s. He was still collecting cards a week or two before he died, planning to add Sidney Crosby and Marc-André Fleury rookie cards to his collection via eBay. I don't know if he ever got the chance to do this. Opening those bins now hurts too much, because Bub never got to retire.

As Bub's little brother, I naturally tried to emulate him. However, baseball card collecting was one activity I couldn't get into as deeply as Bub had. I had cards, maybe a few hundred, but they never captivated me like they did him. Eventually, I gave most of my cards to him, including a Frank Thomas rookie card. My collection mostly came from a board game I got for my birthday one year. I don't remember all the details of how to play, but it was called Strat-O-Matic Baseball. It was a dice and card game where I could play a baseball game. I quickly lost interest and got rid of the board game, but I kept the cards and gave them to my brother . Instead, I turned to other kinds of collecting.

As a kid, I loved collecting and playing with Matchbox cars and Micro Machines, which I still have. They sit on a shelf in my game room (or Megan's Room, as my mom calls it, named after one of my cats). I also collected plastic football and baseball helmets from gumball machines and tiny NFL team mugs.

At one point, my mom and I talked about selling the cards, but we couldn't even start having them appraised. It felt like a monstrous betrayal to him. I don't know if we will ever do anything with them except keep them safe.

We've kept many of the things he held dear. My dad keeps all his tools and uses them regularly, especially for electrical work. It feels like a small way to honor him and his profession. My mom has a box of his drawings and other childhood keepsakes, including a book he filled out each year before school started. I had one, too. They had questions about our best friends, our goals, and what we wanted to be when we grew up. From a very early age, probably eleven or twelve, my brother wrote he wanted to be an electrical engineer.

One of the drawings we have was Bub's favorite. It became the basis for a tattoo. From the day he brought it home, he always said he was going to have it as a tattoo. Years later, I went with him when he got the picture inked onto his shoulder.

Our mom has said many times she refused to believe that it was Bub who was involved in the accident until the person on the other end of the phone mentioned the "Batman tattoo" on his shoulder. It was then that the truth hit home.

Bub's original drawing for his tattoo.

I have a very similar tattoo on my leg, in honor of him. The difference is my tattoo has a yellow halo instead of the baseball cap, along with his dates of birth and death.

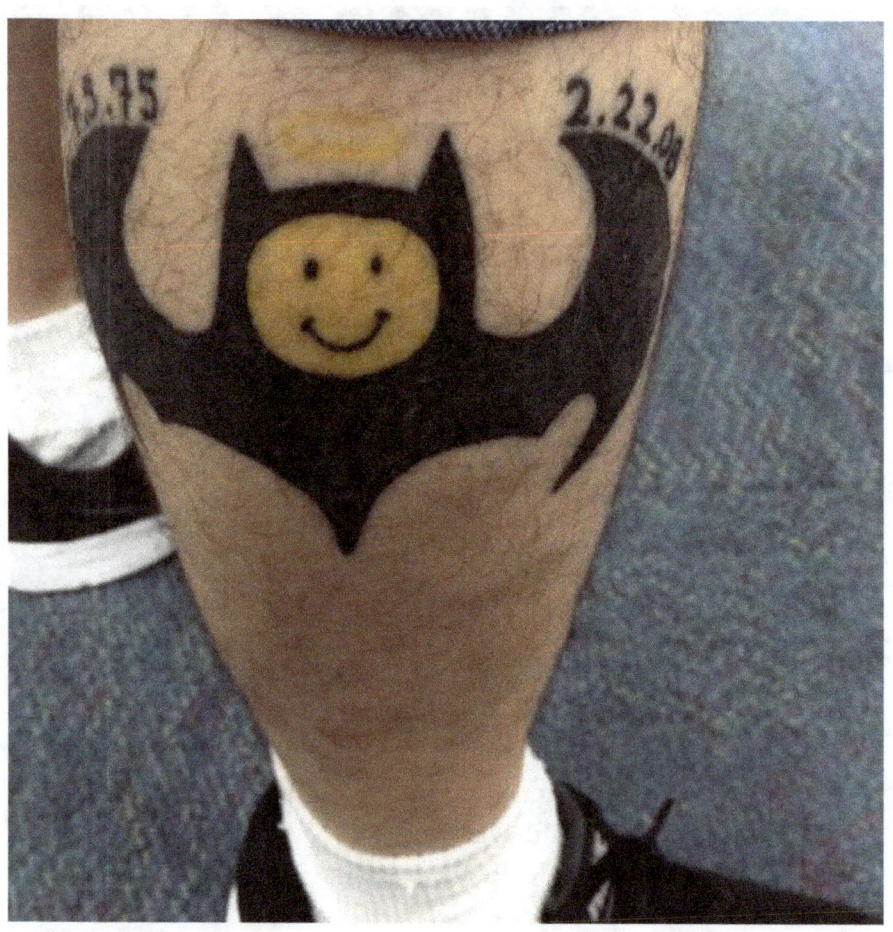

My tattoo, similar to Bub's but with a halo instead of a baseball cap. Unfortunately the halo is not as visible in this picture as I would like, but it is there.

CHAPTER 23

The Bub Light

A light burns, and hope is seen in its glow. We use them as a guide back home for those we know. We who are earthbound still use as a guide as we continue along this row we must hoe. A light for the path. A light to illuminate each laugh. We burn these lights day and night. In honor of one who's been taken from our sight.

In both my house and my parents' house, we have a light that we call "the Bub light." We keep these on at all times to honor him and to keep the light of his life lit inside our hearts. Many bulbs have replaced—as of this writing I think I am on the sixth lamp—but it is always quickly replaced as my superstitious nature believes Bub may get angry with me if it stays out. It has been one thing we've done to honor him daily. We think of him daily, reminisce on him often, and let his light guide us through our daily lives. I really believe the Bub light illuminates the path to our meeting in the next world.

YOUR HEAVEN OR MINE?

Until we meet again
In a happier time
In your heaven
Or in mine
I bid you farewell
But not goodbye
Goodbye is forever
And I know that some day
We will be together

With laughs and smiles,
Until then
I'll wait all the whiles
I'll hold my friend
And hope not
To descend
Until then
When we can begin
All over again
Start fresh and new
Become closer
Than ever have been
So few
You and me
Me and you
Let them see
It will be in heaven
We will be
Even if you don't agree
It'll be a happier time
And we shall be free
No more numbers
Or disease
No more blunders
Only reprieve
No more thunder
Before a rainbow
Only holding on
And never letting go
It can be your heaven
Or it can be mine
As long as it's an eternity
Of you and me
That is just fine.

I have faith that there is another world beyond this, one without the trappings of this life. I have faith I will see my brother once more.

In the meantime, we honor him, such as by ensuring that the Bub lights in our homes never go off for long. Another way we honor him is with fireworks on the fourth of July. In our younger years, we loved fireworks. I think most kids do. We loved to light them and see them go off, exploding. I think as kids, when the adults gave us that thrill, we felt the power in the palm of hands to destroy things. That is a powerful feeling to have, even if it's only paper and pieces of plastic. It is a thrill for sure.

Bub loved fireworks and the fourth of July. Maybe that was because his birthday was the day after. Or maybe it was just because he loved to play with fire. He was almost always the designated fireworks lighter at our family gatherings. Sometimes, though, before these gatherings, Bub and I snuck some stuff off and lit it. One time, he almost blew off his hand with a firecracker. These days we don't do much lighting of fireworks, but we often try to take in a fireworks display somewhere, even if we just watch them on TV. He would be disappointed if we didn't.

Mostly though I think Bub loved fireworks because he loved to celebrate America's birthday and his own birthday together. He was a patriot, that is for sure. When he got his job helping build submarines at General Dynamics, which had government defense contracts, I asked him, "Does it scare you to be building something that could kill people?"

He responded, "I do this to prevent people from wanting to put themselves in a situation where we'd want to attack them."

I took that as a good answer. His birthday is hard sometimes, and Independence Day is hard because while we as a nation may be free, we as Bub's family and friends are never free from the burden of the pain of losing him.

I wrote this in honor of his birthday in 2013.

BIRTHDAY HUG

Happy Birthday brother
It's another year
Another number
And you're gone
And we are left here
All the pain
Still lingering on
It's been awhile
But the pain
Just won't reconcile
An open wound
Just left to fester
The hurt is an emotion
We just can't sequester
Everlasting
And eternal
No prosthesis or casting
No stitching
Could secure
And leave a scar
There'll never be closure
But it's your day
And I hope it's okay
That this is my way
To say happy birthday
I know you're in
Heaven above
But dammit
I need you here
To give you your
Birthday hug.

It wasn't just putting flame to fuses that he loved. He loved many fires. He loved campfires, bonfires, and burning brush after we cleaned up areas of the farm. I think the power of fire fascinated him. Also, with him being an engineer, I think the chemical change that is the true essence of fire was what fascinated him.

* * *

Bub worked his way through college by waiting tables at two different restaurants. He never lost his respect for restaurant workers as he grew more successful and made more money. Any time we went out to eat, he always left a large tip for the server. He always told us to "tip well because it is rarely the servers' fault when something goes wrong with your meal."

I keep that in mind the best I can. Around his birthday every year, I go out to eat or order delivery with either my wife or my mom, and I tip the server or delivery driver an amount that corresponds to what Bub's age would be were he still with us. It has always felt like the right thing to do.

CHAPTER 24

If We Are Lucky

Guns N' Roses covered a Johnny Thunders song called "You Can't Put Your Arms Around a Memory" on their album of cover songs called *The Spaghetti Incident.* I've heard some universal truths in my life. That one may be one of the most painful ones. A lyric from the song goes, "You can't put your arms around a memory, don't try, don't try." So many times I've woken up from dreams where my brother was there. He was alive. He was real. I could touch him, feel his skin, hear his voice. I want to live in these dreams forever. Because when I'm awake, the memories are all I have. I'm blessed to have so many good ones, but some days they aren't enough. And they'll never be enough because the only things left are the tears, the only tangible part of my brother's life becoming the last physical manifestation of the love we shared, the memories we shared, the times we shared and, lastly, the memories that will never get made.

The death of a loved one is the worst kind of robbery. If someone breaks into your home and steals your TV, you can get another one. If someone steals your car, insurance will get you another one. When God steals the life of someone you love, there is no insurance to reimburse you for what's lost. This life has taught me so little about death. It all seems so useless to me. Why are we born just to die? For a few successes in between? For the love we share in between? That seems to be it, to be honest. There sure is an awful lot of pain in between. Without the love, this life wouldn't be worth it. Maybe that's why we are robbed of memories of loved ones, as a reminder of that. I'm thinking about Robin Williams' character in the movie *Good Will Hunting* when he says, "You will have bad times, but they will always wake you up to the stuff you weren't paying attention to."

Maybe that's what it really is all about: just living for the good times and getting through the bad times. If we are lucky, we will have people who love us and support us along the way.

To pull out a quote from a movie that may not have as many life lessons as we think it does on the surface: In *Dazed and Confused*, when they are smoking a joint at the fifty-yard line, Dawson says, "Well, all I'm saying is that I want to look back and say that I did I the best I could while I was stuck in this place. Had as much fun as I could while I was stuck in this place. Played as hard as I could while I was stuck in this place." That was another of Bub's favorite movies.

We do our best every day. Some days we thrive. Some days we survive. Some days memories are made, the core kind that are easy to pull out at any point in time. Some days, probably most days, we couldn't pull a memory from no matter how hard we try. But those are the days— not to be soap opera-y here, but they are the days of our lives, and we must live them. We get through this. Together. Leaning on one another. Sometimes we carry, sometimes we are carried. Sometimes we must let our faith in tomorrow and a grand reunion be the only thing that gets us out of bed in the morning, the only reason we can find that this life isn't just some cosmic joke that we are the butt of.

Nothing I've written in these pages will bring my brother back. Trust me, if words alone could bring him back, he'd be back by now. I've written so many words, not just here, about my grief and struggling with his loss that if they could bring him back, he'd be standing in front of me and I wouldn't have to worry about needing to figure out how to put my arms around a memory.

As I've said, I dream a lot. Sometimes I remember the dreams with such clarity they border on memories rather than just mere dreams, with extreme details being noted. Here is a dream I had in 2018.

In the dream, we, as the human race, were given the power to bring back any person we've ever known who has died. There were rules, though. We could bring back only one person, and they would be back for a period of five years. They would have to live with us the entire time and would not be self-sufficient. No jobs for them or anything; we'd have to provide everything for them. They would know they had been brought back from the dead, but we would be forbidden to ask them anything about their death or the afterlife. There could be no fighting with the person, not so much as a small bickering. They were to be kept from knowing or meeting any other previously dead person who was brought back. We were to make no major changes in our lives: no marriages, divorces, job changes, or moving. We were to tell no one else we brought the person back from the dead; only the person who brought them back would know they had died. All others would be given a kind of amnesia to make them unaware that the person had ever died. Lastly, if we broke any of these rules, they would immediately disappear. Not only would they disappear, but we would forget them, and they would have never existed to us. If we could fulfill these conditions for the five years, we would be guaranteed a spot beside them in heaven. If we weren't successful, the actions of our lives would be judged more critically, and it might be harder for us to get into heaven. However, if we chose not to bring someone back, it would be the regular standards for admission to heaven. God asked us, when this option was given to us, if these conditions were worth more time with the person.

If this scenario were to ever play out, I could see myself being like Nemo in *Mr. Nobody* when his mom leaves. He has three choices: stay with his dad and the life that would lead to, go with the mom and the life that would lead to, or just stand there and refuse to make a decision—and the life that would lead to. As Neil Peart of Rush wrote, "If you choose not to decide, you still have made a choice." But in the scenario in my dream, what would that choice be? I wouldn't be able to make the choice. I'd stand frozen forever—a marble statue, three trolls that saw sunlight, a mosaic stuck in time and place. No decision from this dream would be right. Accepting the terms would mean a huge disruption to life as you knew it. Time with the loved one would balance that out, but would it balance outcompletely? Choosing not to do it could be interpreted as a statement that you didn't care that much about the person in the first place. Choosing not to choose could be seen as a weakness and a lack of commitment.

We, as human animals, hate to be seen as weak and vulnerable. But, if we are lucky, we have people in our lives we can be vulnerable with. Bub was one of those people for me, and I try to be that kind of person for others.

CHAPTER 25

Let It Out

In the years since Bub died, I've been told that I should be over his death. One person told me that just a couple of years after.

"He died three years ago? You should be over it."

Some deaths you don't get over, ever. Writing this memoir will help and has helped. It gives me a document to go back to and see the times we had together. As I grow older and the photographs and memories continue to fade, I will have this book as a refresher. Some deaths, some losses, the circle never closes. The ends keep missing one another. It then becomes a spiral. Our goal in these cases is to slow the spiral, to not let it get to the point that we are out of control. Unfortunately, though, this isn't always possible. We have to lose control or lose our minds. I've certainly lost control. I've beat on the walls with my fists. I've pounded my head against things. The pain and turmoil in my heart that were suffocating my soul had to be let out—bled out, if I may. When the written or spoken word won't suffice, just let go with an inarticulate scream. A Wilhelm scream of sorts. Sometimes you just need to get in your car, find a lonely stretch of highway, and just put the hammer down and turn the music up. Let the speed and the music drown out everything.

SONGS FOR THE PAST

Turn up the radio
Let the classics play
Give me one more chance
To put the future
On tape delay
I know every word

From that other world
I might miss a cue
And fumble a verse
But I'll belt them out
Like a hanging curve
Give me one more song
Let me just stay in the past
Let this be where I belong
Let me pour my soul
Into every line
Let it wash over me
Transplanting my place and time
Turn up the sound
While we're cruising around
Good friends and family
Bonding through the music
Because in the music
We can't be touched
When you keep it inside
You'll never be crushed
It's a beauty that you can never hide
Turn up the radio
When it's playing
Something good
Let the classics flow
Let the memories flood
Just like they should.

Let it out and let go. Or, as the AAs say, "Let go and let God."

CHAPTER 26

Snapshots in Time

Working on this memoir, I've had so many memories that have come bubbling to the surface, like the crude when Pa Clampett was shooting at some game and missed. Some of these can be worked into a longer narrative. Others, though, I think need their own place. These snapshots in time, as I will call them, are often a sentence, maybe three, about a particular moment caught in time that this writing has rattled free.

1. The first one I'll list is maybe one of the funniest things my brother ever did. First time he met my first wife; we were at my house where I was living with my friend Dan. Audrey was talking a mile a minute because she is the nervous type. At the end of one of her sentences, she said, "If I am talking too much, just tell me to shut up." In a perfect deadpan, he turned to her and said, "Shut up." She did.

2. Bub, Dan, and I would often rent *NCAA Football* for whatever game system we had, then play it all weekend. Bub would always be Ohio State, Dan would play as Pitt, and I would be Notre Dame. We would buy a tray of pizza from DeCesare's or DiCarlo's and eat it all weekend.

3. One time Bub was changing the oil in his car and forgot to set the emergency brake. It was a standard shift. He went in the house, and the transmission popped out of gear. The car went rolling down through the yard. Luckily for him, our Grandpap had recently placed some large round bales of hay where the car ended up. The car hit the hay. No damage, but the front end was imprinted on the hay.

4. Once—this was after Bub passed away—I called his cat AJ "Fat-J." Two days later, my PlayStation 3 got fried from a bolt of lightning hitting the ground outside the cabin my then-wife and I were vacationing in.

5. I remember going to Bub's house at three in the morning to get ready to go watch the implosion of Three Rivers Stadium. He lived on

Mount Washington in Pittsburgh at the time, which gave us a magnificent view after only a short walk.

6. Bub hated macaroni and cheese.

7. When we were kids, we weren't allowed to get up from the table unless we cleaned our plates. Bub would take my vegetables off my plate and eat them when our dad wasn't looking because he liked them and I didn't.

8. The first time we heard Nirvana, I thought at first that they were called "Nerd-wanna" because I didn't hear the DJ correctly. Then the opening guitar of "Smells Like Teen Spirit" played. We were blown away and were instant fans. Because we were the first out of everyone we knew to hear Nirvana, we always said we discovered them.

9. When we stayed at our Grandpap Chase's house, we got up to typical teenage dickens. I won't explain because the statute of limitations may not be in effect yet.

10. We went camping once with our cousins Jay, Freddie, and Ivan and a bottle of Southern Comfort. Freddie walked through the fire like a dumbass.

11. The ponds at our Uncle Dave's strip mine would ice over in winter, and we cousins used to go play ice hockey there. Bub was always sent out to check the ice. Mostly because he was the lightest, but also because he was the bravest of us.

12. During the blizzard of 1993, we were pounded with three feet of snow. We lived next to my grandparents' farm, so my dad used their front loader to scoop the snow up and make a pile. Bub and I took advantage to build an igloo that was ten feet high, maybe more. We then used our dad's mini shovel to dig through it, creating a ice slide down through the middle of it on our sleds, which led to us going down over the hill between our house and our grandparents' house.

13. I went with Bub the day he went to pick up his brand-new Mustang. His dream car. He was so proud that day, as I was of him.

14. One day the phone rang, and Bub and I learned that the terrible things people do on TV sometimes happen to people in real life. Our dad answered the phone. He screamed, "WHAT!?" Bub asked, "Is it Grandpap? Did something happen to Grandpap?" Dad shook his head.

When he hung up, he told us, "Little Dude is dead. Someone shot him." Someone had murdered one of my mom's and dad's best friends at a keg party over a stupid argument that meant nothing. Bub and I looked at each other and hugged. Then we cried.

15. We had a close call with a tornado once. My mom and I were hiding, scared to death. Bub stood in the kitchen window and watched the tornado come down our road and then leap over our trailer.

16. We went to the dog races in Wheeling one New Year's Eve. Bub bet 7–5 quinella on every race because that is his birthday, 7/5/75.

17. Once we went to Aunt Pat's house in a snowstorm to watch the Steelers game. They were playing Green Bay that day, his second favorite team. The car slid off the road. Luckily we were buckled in and weren't hurt, only shaken.

18. Bub's emails to me usually started with the salutation "Hey Dick."

19. Our usual greeting upon seeing each other was to flip one another off.

20. Once, Dan and I were lost in Pittsburgh. I called Bub at his job in Connecticut and gave him a landmark, and he gave us turn-by-turn directions to get out of the city and on our way home.

21. Bub made me try alligator meat. That stuff was terrible.

22. When Bub's work took him to Virginia, I visited him there, and we went to an aquarium. Bub wanted to smack a stingray because one had just killed Steve Irwin the day before.

23. In ninth grade, I was on the basketball team, and I got into a fight during a game. Bub was standing up in the crowd and screaming, "KICK HIS ASS, ROBB!" because he was as tired of seeing the guy take cheap shots at me as I was tired of receiving them.

24. He was the best baseball coach I ever had. He would sit in the stands and watch the opposing pitcher, then come up to me between at-bats and tell me what he was doing, what to look for, and how to approach the next pitch. His advice was always dead on.

25. Bub and I went to Ozzfest together, and I saw Slayer for the first time. Bub had seen them multiple times. They were amazing live. Better than Ozzy.

26. The summer after that Ozzfest, summer 2002, I worked on a cruise ship. The last cruise I worked docked across the river from where Bub was working. He picked me up to bring me back to Ohio. On the way home, we passed a boat that wasn't on a trailer, just up on blocks, sitting along the highway with a woman sunbathing on the back. We turned to each other and said, "What the fuck did I just see?" at the same exact time.

27. Earlier that summer, I had a break from the ship and needed a haircut. Bub took me to get one. I was going on and on about how attractive I thought the stylist was. He looked me dead in the eye and said, "You haven't seen many women lately, have you?" I shut up about her.

28. This one time, I was trying to sneak up the steps at our Grandpap's house. Bub wasn't fooled. He jumped out from around the corner and aimed a kick at me. He misjudged the distance and hit me right in the face with his shoe-clad foot. Blood gushed immediately. I thought he broke my nose. So did he. He thought he was going to get into big trouble. I didn't tattle. Told our mom I slipped on the steps.

29. I think every younger sibling has a story like this next one. Bub and I were wrestling around in the living room. He had this wiry strength, and he threw me off a little too vigorously and I fell down and hit my right ear on the corner of the base of the couch. It was one of those old couches I think everyone had in those years, the one with the cushions with the sawmill scene. The frames of those things were solid wood. I hit my ear right on the corner of the leg; blood was running down my neck and into my shirt. He begged me to tell our mom I'd just fallen and he'd done nothing to cause it. Again I didn't tell.

30. We were bored and wanted pizza. Bub didn't have his license yet, so we walked to Hammondsville to get pizza at a little place called Cliff's. We got our pizza and walked home. On the way home, we saw a snake lying on the path. Bub liked snakes. I am deathly scared of them. He picked up a stick and teased it. It got pissed. Raised up and struck at the stick. When that didn't stop Bub, the snake came after him. I've mentioned that Bub ran track. I did not. He took off running and was past me in a flash. I ran after him and kept running as hard and for as long as I could. He had to stop running because he couldn't stop laughing.

31. We built a fort in back of our house, in the cow field. We wanted to sleep overnight in it but were never given permission to. It was made of old couch cushions and a tarp.

32. One time I borrowed one of Bub's cassettes without his permission. So he told our dad I'd been cussing on the bus. He then laughed as I got my ass beat for no reason. It was one of the few times in my life I could claim innocence when it comes to swearing.

33. Bub dropped a pencil inside the *USS Virginia,* the submarine he was helping build in Connecticut, when he was writing down some dimensions. He thought this was hilarious.

34. One time, after a domestic dispute with our dad, I called Bub in Pittsburgh and told him what happened. He showed up at our house twenty-five minutes later. It was normally a fifty- or sixty-minute drive.

35. When our grandpap Chase was getting ready to pass away, I called Bub in Pittsburgh and he made it to our uncle Cecil's house in about thirty minutes. Same fifty- or sixty-minute drive.

36. The first time our family had a cell phone, Bub tried to trick my friend Josh by calling him from his driveway. When Josh answered, we said we were just leaving our house. But Josh said he saw us in his driveway. Safe to say, it didn't work.

37. I watched him run in the Dover Invitational track meet. He was leading by a lot in the 1600-meter race. He made the turn and was on the backstretch when the wind picked up and was slamming into his face. It was like watching him hit a physical wall and then bounce back.

38. Every once in a while, Bub would rub snuff. Grandpap Chase also did. But Grandpap called modern snuff "pussy shit"; he used this old stuff in a tin can that was like a powder. He offered my brother some, but Bub couldn't hang with it. Grandpap thought it was hilarious.

39. The last time I saw Bub, he helped me pick out a suede coat. I was wearing it the last time we hugged. It has never been washed.

40. One time Bub refused to go to the Blackburn family get-together on Christmas Day. Our dad was pissed. Bub said, "The family hates me anyway."

41. We used to have Monopoly marathons in the evenings during vacation Bible school at Aunt Pat's. I feel like Bub always won.

42. One time, Bub saw a bear outside Aunt Pat's and Uncle Dave's house. He told everyone what he had seen, but no one believed him. Then Uncle Dave's mom, who lived just up the road, called and told them a bear was in her trash. Uncle Dave went up to her house and found the tracks. Bub had a nice I-told-you-so on that one.

43. Bub used to deliver pizza for a local place in Wellsville. One night he came home and told me a blonde had opened her door naked. Didn't go into more detail. I have always wondered what his tip was. Or perhaps she got the tip.

44. One time, when I was maybe seven and Bub was eleven, we built the ugliest snowman imaginable. It was asymmetrical, made of dirty snow, and had the weirdest face ever. We were still proud of it.

45. One time Bub and I went to Pittsburgh to go to the mall, but we couldn't find it. We stopped at a gas station, and Bub asked, "Where's Century 21 Mall?" The cashier looked at us like we were nuts. The mall's name was Century 3. We were less than a quarter mile from it.

46. Bub played football for one year in high school, his sophomore year. He was really good at it. He was on the junior varsity team, and he was an everything man. He played receiver, running back, defensive back, linebacker, and kick returner. I believe he even threw a few passes. Watching him play every game, I was always amazed to see him carry defensive players that were probably twice his weight, moving entire piles of humanity. My God, he was amazing.

47. Bub was steadfastly determined to get out of the Ohio Valley, which he called "a hellhole." For me, it is just home.

48. Bub had an amazing amount of patience. One time he was working on his car. I'm not sure what he was doing, but it wasn't going right. He just kept trying and trying until he got it right. Me, or our dad, we would have been cussing up a storm and throwing stuff. Bub was just determined to figure it out.

49. Bub loved *The Sopranos* and *Lost*, and he used to talk my ear off about them. I was lost because I had no idea what he was talking about. But his passion for those shows was amazing.

50. Every time Bub and I played *Golden Tee Golf*, the roller golf arcade game, he kicked my ass. If there had been a professional circuit for that game, he could have been on it.

51. Going bowling with him was fascinating. He put every ounce of his weight into each roll, making the ball fly down the alley, frame after frame. I think he secretly wanted to shatter a pin, because he rolled the ball as hard as he could every single time.

52. In social situations, I think the only times Bub truly came out of his shell and his personality shone through was when he was drinking. I think he loved that but hated it as well.

53. Jay's songs that he plays in Bub's honor when he's intoxicated are "Two Suns in the Sunset" by Pink Floyd and "Subdivisions" by Rush.

54. Bub had a huge number of band T-shirts. Our mom turned them into a quilt for our cousin Lisa.

55. One time I tweeted at the producer and the DJ of our favorite morning radio program asking for a shout-out for Bub on the anniversary of his death. The DJ actually did it, leading into Led Zeppelin's "All of My Love." The producer DMed me afterwards to say, "I can't believe Randy did that. He never does that."

56. One winter, Bub and I built perhaps the ugliest snowman ever. It was still fun, though. Yes, twice. We were not expert snowman builders.

57. One time we were fishing in the creek, and we caught a snapping turtle. I took off running because it was coming after us. Bub just coolly picked it up by the tail and threw it back in the water.

58. I remember making pizza sandwiches over a campfire Bub and I built when we went camping at our uncle Roger's cabin on an island in the Ohio River.

59. Bub had no problem getting up for school. I am not a morning person and would always get up about five minutes before the bus came. One morning he tried to trick me by setting all the clocks ahead. But I knew right away that it was a trick, and I took my time. I told him, "If I'm late, so are you." Which was true, because if we missed the bus, he had to drive us both to school.

60. We went fishing once with our cousins Tommy and Ivan. We were walking down the path to the spot, and Bub decided to prank me and yell, "Snake!" I took off running back up the path and about five hundred feet down the dirt road. Ivan was not far behind me. Bub and Tommy were standing there laughing their asses off.

61. I remember how excited and happy Bub was when he got his letterman's jacket for Christmas. I got a bike that we had seen at an auction. Our uncle Dave had won the auction on it and said he was giving it to his nephew on his side of the family. I was devastated, so it was an enormous surprise when I actually got the bike. Our dad took us somewhere on Christmas Eve, and when we returned, in the kitchen was a blanket draped over something. Bub and I pulled it off together. My bike was there, and his jacket was on the handlebars. I was ecstatic. He was more so.

62. Bub of course agreed to be the best man at my first wedding, which was always fitting because he was always one of the best men I've ever known. Right there on equal footing with our Grandpap Chase.

63. His friends at the restaurant he worked at gave him the nickname "Scoboki" because when they asked him where he was from, he said, "The middle of nowhere." Scoboki supposedly meant that in Japanese. Research has shown me that it means, well, nothing at all. I now have a kitten named this.

64. We went to see the band Live at Starlake Amphitheater on their Secret Samadhi tour. "Whatever milk means to you."

65. One night we played video games all night and kept trying to call in to a radio station to request Smashing Pumpkins' "Bullet with Butterfly Wings." Bub finally got through and requested it. When the DJ played it, he mentioned other people's names, but not ours! Dick move, DJ. Dick move.

66. Bub loved ice cream, chocolate being his favorite. We often bought tubs of Neapolitan. He and our dad would try to get to the chocolate first. Which was fine with Mom and I; she prefers vanilla, and I like strawberry. That dude could have subsisted on ice cream alone, I think.

67. Speaking of ice cream, I think the only times we voluntarily went to our grandma Blackburn's house was when we wanted an ice cream

cone, because she always had some. So we would just walk over the hill to get them.

68. Bub displayed complete stoicism in all situations. I don't know I ever saw him lose control of his emotions.

69. I was talking to him in the checkout line at Walmart after he was offered a job in Connecticut. He said they wanted him to submit a salary proposal. He said he was going to ask for "a G a week." I said "Wow. You think they'll pay you that much?" He said, "That's just the start." That much money seemed unfathomable to me. They ended up countering his 52K with 55K. So he even underestimated it as well.

70. I remember two-a.m. Taco Bell runs on Sunday nights when they had tacos for 39 cents.

71. I remember the time I asked the pizza shop Bub worked for to make me a cheese stuffed crust calzone. He said, "They told me to tell you to never fucking ask for that again. It's too hard to do."

72. I remember the look of pride on Bub's face when I graduated from college. That memory is etched into my brain.

73. One day in elementary school, I got off the bus and a snake crawled across my foot. I kicked it up in the air and sprinted to the top of the yard, where Bub was standing. I told him what happened. He, of course, went to look for the snake and was disappointed not to find it.

74. Bub had a little stuffed dog named Ralph. Our parents still have it.

75. When Bub had his first time off in two years, another bucket list item for him was going to Miami Beach. I think he was there a day or two and then a hurricane came. Of course, it was Hurricane Ivan. Our cousin Ivan was always the most, well, I'll say ornery of our bunch.

CHAPTER 27

Mother

B ecause she is our mom, she gets her own chapter. Most moms have a special bond with their children. Ours is no different. My brother and I always considered our mom the best. Even with the challenges she faced raising us, no matter what, she always loved us. Even when we made mistakes. Our mom never berated us or anything. I can't remember a single time that she raised her voice to either of us in genuine anger. Maybe once or twice out of pure fear, but I think that is completely different.

Below are the words handwritten by our mom about her son. Following are the actual handwritten pages so you can see the love poured out directly onto the page. From her soul to her heart through her brain, passing along the nerves to the fingers to be traced by the pen, her words and her true heart are on display.

I was always a little jealous of their relationship. Not saying my mom and I had or have a poor relationship, because we absolutely don't. It is amazing, and I wouldn't change anything about it. There always seemed to be just something extra between the two of them, just a little more special. I don't know if it was a first-born child thing or not. But it was there, and even as a small child I could recognize it even if I couldn't identify what it was. Perhaps some motherly instinct told her, deep down in those places where no light ever shines in our souls, that he needed a lifetime of love because the life he was going to live would be truncated. Since I have outlived him, all the love I received and am receiving from mom is spread out over a longer period.

Nothing can spoil a mother's love. Nothing replaces a mother's love. Losing a brother has been nearly unbearable for me. Losing a child, though—my god, you're not just losing a living being that you love; you're losing a part of you. A piece of every mother is passed to her children. When they die before their mother, a piece of the mother dies too.

Without further ado, here are our mom's words.

* * *

My son—Jerry was my first-born child. I remember the day I found out I was going to have a baby. I was so excited. I was ready to be a mother.

Most of my pregnancy I would be alone. We lived in Norfolk, VA at the time. Jerry Sr. seemed to be away a lot. He was in the navy. So it was just me and my baby. I remember talking to him, I just knew it was a boy. I told him I would love and take care of him always.

So Boo—that was my nickname for him—and I spent a lot of time together alone. His first two weeks of life, he would sleep on my stomach because he had colic, and that was the only way I could give him relief. He got over that, and he would just smile and coo so much. He loved to kick his legs a lot. He was a very active baby. He learned to stand on his feet when he was six months old. Started to walk soon after that.

When he was six months old, we went to the Ohio State Fair. His dad won a big black dog for him. We had him laying on a car bed. He was kicking it, causing it to move up and down. A guy thought it was a real dog, I told him no my baby was kicking it. He was having a ball with that dog.

He was just a happy little boy. We grew so close. He went everywhere with me. When his teeth started to come in, he would chew on a piece of wood from a Lincoln log set. He got his first black eye when was two years old. He fell and hit the corner of a coffee table chasing his pet bunny Uncle Wayne got him. He called him "Boo." That was his first pet.

He was a fast learner, he'd pick up stuff so easy. His first word was "Mommy". He was so short that he had to stand on the top of my feet to go to the potty. So my mistake, "big boy toilet," he wouldn't use a potty because they were for babies.

He was the firstborn grandson for Robert and Ada. His grandpa was so proud of him. I remember he got him a truck and a sandbox to play in.

There are so many memories of my son. I cherish them all. We were so close he became my whole world. Of course, he was my center of attention for four years and then I got pregnant with my second son. When I told him he was going to get a brother or a sister, he was so excited. Of course, everyone told him he was getting a sister, so he thought he was getting a sister. The first time he saw his brother he seemed sad, but I told him "just think: he'll play in the dirt with you, play ball, do things boys like to do and girls don't. And besides, with a brother, that means twice the toys." He liked that idea and took his little brother under his wing. He would not let anyone hurt his brother. They grew up to be so close. So then it became the three of us doing everything together. Jerry Sr. was not very active in their childhood. I always told him he would regret it, and I believe he does now.

I saw my son grow up from a small baby boy to a man. I saw him fulfill his dreams and goals. I am so proud of my sons.

And then, in a flash, he was gone. I don't like to talk about that much. I just want to remember him as a very intelligent, loving, caring, hardworking young man.

The last time I saw and talked to Bub, we were watching a Pens game, and I made a comment about the goalie "Fleury." I said "he sucks."

He said, "Yeah, but he's going to be a great goalie one of these years." I follow him and he is a great goalie, Boo, you got that one right.

That night we talked about, of all things, death. He told me his wishes and how he needs to set some new goals for the future. Then the next day he left. He gave me a hug and said, "I love you, Mom." I thought that was weird because when I told him I loved him, he would respond with "yep." I watched him drive away, never to see him or hear his voice again.

The night he passed away, I was woken from sleep and I heard his voice screaming "Mommy." So my son's first spoken word was Mommy, and it would be his last. Rest in peace, my son.

Mom and Bub together in Virginia circa 1975.

Mom and Bub at the Connecticut River.

* * *

Here is a link to a video on YouTube:

https://www.youtube.com/watch?v=O-JlnC79C7M

It's a montage of photos and music Mom created for me as a birth-day gift a few years after we lost Bub. It is hard for me to watch, I can only do it on occasion but please check it out, it is the best example of the bond my brother and I shared, and the one we had with our mom.

It is humbling how, when we look back at old pictures, we see the smiles and laughter and think to ourselves, *I was happy in that moment.* We try to place ourselves in that frame of mind, imagining what it was like to be the younger self in the photograph. We long to regain the feeling that made us smile for the camera—especially when the photo includes someone we have lost.

We see the shared joy, and we sit with the sadness of knowing how limited those moments truly were. We didn't realize, in that instant, that tragedy was lying in wait. That a simple shutter click would one day hold all that remained of that happiness.

Pictures, even the happiest ones, can wound us. Nostalgia is its own special kind of pain.

CHAPTER 28

Funerals Suck

We had a funeral for my brother, but his body was not present. It was not great. Funerals suck. I am certain there isn't a person who may read this who doesn't agree with that statement. They aren't fun; they suck. They are never a celebration of a life, and they usually feature a religious person who barely has any connection to the deceased standing in front of everyone reading the same tired Bible quotes that we have all heard a thousand times if we have been to enough funerals—and one is more than enough if I'm being completely honest. I'm sure Bible quotes give some people comfort, me being one of them sometimes. However, they are mostly just annoying to me, especially at my brother's funeral, because he was not a religious person. He didn't attend church outside of vacation Bible school when we were kids with my Aunt Pat. We and cousins Lisa and Jay (Jerry; yes, another Jerry) and various other cousins would stay at Aunt Pat's house and then pile into her car. Some of us sat on others' laps, which is unheard of today, but it happened back in the '80s and early '90s. Funerals, though, they suck, especially if you are one of the core family members and are given the honored position of sitting in the first row. You sit there and receive everyone's grief while attempting to grieve yourself. It is just stupid. To use the modern parlance, I give it 0 stars, would not recommend.

I remember that procession of grief clearly because of how much it sucked. I remember two other parts of the funeral. One was thinking about how pissed my brother was going to be at me for breaking a promise I made to him years before his death. I think we may have been going to a Pirates game. I remember the conversation taking place in his car. He made me swear, "At my funeral, I want you to play 'South of Heaven' and 'Hell Awaits' by Slayer." I made the promise. When we were arranging the music, my cousin Joyce's daughter Amber was making the CD with the songs (I'm sure all illegally downloaded). When I went to the funeral home the next day and listened to the music, there was no Slayer. I was pissed.

I asked, "Where is the Slayer?"

Someone responded, "We didn't think that was appropriate."

I said, "I don't give a shit. I promised Bub I'd have those songs played at his funeral."

No one cared, so my promise was broken. Which probably led to the other thing I remember about the funeral. In the middle of the "sermon," a disturbingly loud, clear, and long train whistle sounded. Again and again and again. My cousin Jay said, "I just assumed Bub was fucking with us and when it quit, he'd come walking through the door. I just keep expecting him to walk through the door. We've been through everything together. It seems impossible to go through this without him."

My friend Dan added, "I think that was Bub, just letting us know he's okay."

One other thing I hated about it—this is probably not even relevant, but I want to say it: After the funeral, we went to a hall to have dinner. One of our aunts by marriage came up to me and said, "I need to get some pictures of you. I don't have any recent pictures of you."

I looked her dead in the eyes and said, "I don't think this is the fucking time."

If I had a funeral for him today, first, it wouldn't be at a funeral home. Not a fucking chance. Those places suck. Most likely I would decide to have it at Jefferson State Park, which is where our high school cross-country team had their practices and home races. Part of the celebration of his life would be to have everyone capable walk the path of the course for the races, so we could one last time walk in his footsteps. If we did this in a pavilion, I would hang some of his concert shirts, posters, and other band memorabilia from the rafters. I'd have his favorite music playing. I think my mom still has his CD collection somewhere, and with a subscription to Apple Music, I could easily reinvent a playlist of his favorite music. We could see if we could contact the local humane society and have some kittens and cats there that would be up for adoption. We would definitely have fireworks, a lot of fireworks, because, as I've said earlier, fireworks were one of his favorite things. He loved them and fire, so I think a bonfire would be ideal. I'd love to see food that he loved, some sort of buffet of seafood, which is what he loved most. Especially lobster and crab legs.

I'd love to have a book where people could write some memories or anecdotes about his life or have a microphone so anyone who wanted to could get up and speak to tell stories about him. We could also set up a donation box for people to donate to an animal shelter to help rescue cats. It would be a hell of a lot better than sitting in a funeral home.

In time, I would love to organize a race, a 5 or 10K to raise money for a scholarship for underprivileged kids at our alma mater who grew up in a similar financial situation.

I feel that this would be a better way to honor my brother than sitting in a funeral home.

CHAPTER 29

Breakdown

Grieving sucks. It's not a statement I think anyone will disagree with. In these days of a continual rift between the people of this country, I think everyone can still agree with that statement. Grief is terrible because there are no roadmaps, no signposts, nothing that can help us through the process in a nice linear fashion. Everyone has advice on how to deal with it. I heard advice from all quarters on how to get through the grief of losing my brother. But I know something now that I probably assumed I knew before. It is all bullshit. All advice is bullshit. I don't mean that it is unwelcome advice or that it is coming from a terrible place, although some of it is bad and appears malicious. I mean it's bullshit because what works for one person will not work for someone else. Maybe my assertion is harsh. If it is, oh well. We all have to do it our way and in our own time. In the aftermath of this tragedy, people gave me a lot of advice that was usually well-meaning, if unhelpful.

My wife told me to go to therapy. I did. I found a counselor. I went a few times. I hated it. It didn't seem to help. The counselor seemed to be more in awe of the tragedy than concerned about helping me through it. She asked what, looking back now, I think were inappropriate questions about the details. Maybe she thought they were pertinent. Maybe she was just being nosy. I don't know. I stopped going. Audrey wasn't happy with me, but it didn't help me. I didn't think it made sense to keep going. I internalized all my grief. All my sadness was turning me inside. I was having nightmares, as I described previously. I had trouble sleeping, which made me moody. My blood sugar was out of control. I didn't care and ate whatever I wanted, hoping to join my brother in death. The pain would end with death, even if all that was there to greet me was eternal darkness. That was preferable to a world without my brother. It wasn't only my grief that tormented me. It was seeing how hurt my mom was. Knowing that she was in so much pain crushed me. Still crushes me to this day. My mom has always been my best friend. My entire life, she has been there for me. Never wavering. Never. When I was a poor college student, I wrote a poem for her as a Mother's Day present. Here it is:

HERO

36 hours
And a cloud of dust
Here comes the baby
And he don't weigh that much
In order to survive
He's going to need more than love
He needs someone that will match his blood
Two and a half months premature
Whether he'd survive
No one was really sure.
Then here comes the hero of this story
Still weary from delivery
She gave her blood
To her son, whom she already loved.
Fast forward now
To a later time
She in the stands
He on the field
Her, his number one fan,
Hardly ever missed a game
No matter the sports name
Always there
With the loudest cheer,
Then one day

In a flash

Everything was no longer ok

He, lying there in a pool of blood

She, knowing what needed to be done,

Tear drops his eye

Looking up, he thinks,

"Mommy, am I going to die?"

On now, to a later time

He, off to college

His time to shine

Her, at home

Her baby gone.

Thinks he is

Such a big man

Doesn't really understand

How truly cruel the world can be

On the phone every night

He thinks he is talking to

The love of his life.

But suddenly light

Turns to dark.

Mommy, your little boy

Has a broken heart.

This thought just won't leave

He just can't live

With broken heart disease.

He is going insane

He feels so ashamed

He feels he's lost the game

He takes the blame

For the shame

That came

With not using his brain.

Together, they got through

Two best friends
Doing for each other
Whatever they could do.
Now things are better
She says, "I love you"
He says, "whatever"
But if you will notice
Both phrases have eight letters
He's just a little quirky
Some might even say dorky
For the things he thinks of,
But this is his way of expressing love.
Everyone has heroes
And when they come around, fear goes away
Some use athletes, actors or the like
And that's ok,
But he, he don't need any of them
He spells hero a different way
M-O-M.

I hope this conveys thoroughly the emotions I feel about her and why her pain was my pain.

I was spiraling out of control. My depression was deepening. I didn't know what to do to pull myself out of it. I continued to mask all my pain. It was becoming impossible for me to go to work at the adolescent hospital because every time I went there, I was reminded of how I got the news when I was on the clock there. I left that job and got a new part-time job. That didn't help all that much either. I felt like it was a drag anchor. I had written nothing in a long time, maybe a year or more, except taking the poem above about Mom and amending it to be about Bub. It ended with his nickname spelled out: BUB. That is all I remember about it, though, because I do not have it saved anywhere. I think if my mom has the brochure or whatever it is called that they give you at funerals, it will be on there. She had it printed on there.

At the urging of some of my friends, most notably Becky and Heather, I started writing again. They wanted me to express myself in the way I know. They encouraged me to write something as an outlet. I remember sitting at work, in the office of the house of the gentleman I take care of. My head down. Tears streaming down my face. Sweat on my brow. It was the eleventh of August, 2008. It wasn't a particularly hot day that day. But my emotional temperature was redlining. I was shaking. I sat before the computer, Microsoft Word open. I started to type, trying to pour out as much emotion as possible. I wanted to cut that vein, bleed myself of the pain as best I could. This is what I came up with in my semi-self-hypnotic state. I think it was close to a stream-of-consciousness piece.

UGLY TRUTH

I ain't dead

But I'm dying

I ain't sad

But I'm crying

I ain't worth much

But I'm trying

I ain't there

And you ain't here

But right now, it doesn't matter

Because I don't want to be

Anywhere.

I'm alive

But I'm not living

I'm tired and beaten

But I'm not giving

I'm alone

But I'm not scared

I have a phone

But it's not ringing

I feel nothing
So I guess this is apathy
I just live day by day
You can get me to smile
But not get me happy
I wish I could remember
And live the rest of my life
In last December
Back when I thought I knew
What pain really was
Now I don't have to think
It's everlasting in my heart
There are no words
Just the silence
And I know
Because I am listening
And I just hope it's something
That I'm missing
This is pain at its widest breadth
I have people but I feel so alone
And I wish for death
With every breath.
But I still just get up every day
And live and being fake
In every way
And I block the truth at every turn
Because this is one truth
I never wanted to learn.

After I finished this, I felt some relief. The ending is a lie, though. I knew it was a lie. I could not admit to anyone about how I had killed my brother with a thought. That didn't come until eight or nine years later. I remember breaking down while I was taking a shower. I screamed, cried, punched the wall in the shower. But even that wasn't enough. I banged my head off the wall. Audrey came running into the room, and I was just screaming repeatedly that I had killed him. That I deserved to die. That I was guilty of killing him. I fell out of the shower and just lay there, curled into the fetal position, weeping as hard as I had when I found out the news. Audrey couldn't handle my emotions. She called my mom, and she immediately came to my house. I was still crying when she got there. I couldn't bring myself to admit to her at first what felt I had done. I had to have Audrey tell her because my shame locked my mouth closed tighter than a bank vault.

My mom insisted, "It was God that took him. He needed him more than we did, apparently."

Her words and her comfort helped in that moment, but over the years, it has always been in the back of my mind that it was my fault. I also always felt that my brother was more loved by the family. I have often felt like an afterthought throughout my life. That may only be because I have so many cousins on my mom's side of the family. I was easily just lost in the crowd of faces at every family gathering. I even often quoted a movie I saw after Bub's death, *Walk Hard: The Legend of Dewey Cox*: "Wrong kid died."

At the end of 2017, when the next anniversary of his death was approaching, I was spiraling down and down into a deep depression. Approaching a decade without him, my self-imposed guilt over his death became all-consuming. I couldn't sleep. I was lying in bed at work, tossing and turning, hating myself more and more with each passing breath. I wished I could just stop that breath and get the death I so richly deserved. The rage I was focusing inward on myself was consuming me. To find some relief, I picked up my phone and tapped out these words:

THE HIDDEN CRIMES OF MAN

I can no longer live with this deceit

It's time that I must admit defeat

I am here to lay my sword at your feet

I tried to be strong, but it turns out I'm weak

I tried for more but just couldn't keep

"HEY DICK"

I looked for purpose in between the lines
I stared so long I missed all the signs
Persecute me for I committed so many crimes
I forgot what I couldn't remember so many times
I forged lies with so many "I'm fines"

I couldn't see but for the trees
I fell down upon the streets
Scraped and scabbed up my knees,
I wondered the purpose of this disease
How many times can we live as we bleed?

I wondered about life without you
I questioned what I would do
I wanted the pain that's true
I wanted to feel my life gone askew
I just didn't care how, what, or with who.

I accept all the blame
Leave it at my doorstep in my name
It's my fault I'll never be the same
My fault there's only flicker to where there used to be
    flame
I am forever consumed by my shame

I accept if you hate me
It's the way things should be
I just had to see
I would hate me
I do hate me for how I wanted things to be

I wish I could take it back
My repugnant selfish act
I can't and that's a fact

I long for all the things I lack
I am consumed for having no tact
I will never forgive myself for that.

The act of writing this poem didn't absolve me of my guilt, but it gave me a momentary release, a small breath in the suffocating darkness. Yet, as I lay there, staring at the words on my screen, I hoped there was forgiveness for myself in my heart. I felt my brother would never forgive me.

CHAPTER 30

Grief Is Redundant

I keep returning to the topic of grief. I know it's redundant. But so is grief. For many of us who grieve, there is some point of our grief we constantly return to, whether it be dreams we have of the gone loved one, a memory from when they were alive, a point in the immediate aftermath of their death, or somewhere else along their or your life's timeline. For each of us, it's going to be individual and unique, and very personal. Obviously, the point I returned to was: I killed my brother with a thought. For my wife, it's dreams where her Pappap appears not to be doing well in the dreams. I'm sure there is some interpretation there that could make sense. Perhaps I just don't see it. I don't know. It's clear to me that grief overall doesn't make much sense. I don't mean why we grieve; that is clear. We hurt. We miss the person. Their absence leaves a gaping hole inside of us. The love is still present, but it turns a duller shade of red as time passes. Not that it tarnishes in time, but it washes out. That hole widens in time as we age and mature because the natural course of time stretches what's inside of us, and the memories and love that filled those gaps is lost. We grieve as much for the memories we don't get to make and the love we don't get to share as we do for the pain of the missing and the loss itself.

We attempt to hold ourselves together. We try to fill the gaps in a variety of ways. I filled mine with self-loathing. I filled myself with words in my poetry about missing my brother. Those completely inadequate substitutes for the genuine love and the lost opportunity to make more memories made me bitter. And they still do. I don't know who to aim that bitterness at, though. Usually it's myself because of the thought I had and expressed. Occasionally, it's God. Now and then, it's my brother. At times, the bartender is the culprit. The train conductor is sometimes the one. Sometimes it's the judge who sentenced Bub to jail, making him lose his job. Sometimes it's the job that lied to him. They told him he would still have his job when he got out, but then they reneged. The bitterness is like the taste of the blood all those named above have on our hands. No matter how often I take a drink of something to get that taste out of my mouth, it never washes away. Temporary relief may happen, but the bitter taste is never completely gone. I hope that by writing this I can wash that taste out of my mouth once and for all.

Often we say that it's about the journey and not the destination. However, here, both are of equal importance. It's been just as important to tell the story of my brother and his untimely death as it has been to absolve myself of the irrational guilty feelings that I've harbored since he died. I don't need people to tell me the feelings are irrational. I know they are. That still doesn't stop them from coming and being extremely persuasive. Somehow, irrational thoughts sometimes find an easier foothold in a person's consciousness than rational thoughts. Especially when the events themselves make no sense at all.

Nothing prepares you for grief. No matter what. Even if the person lost has long suffered from a terminal illness and you can tell them goodbye, you still aren't prepared. When our mom's dad died in 1998, we knew for months that he was sick and could go at any time. He was ninety-five years old. He lived a good long life. But that didn't make the grieving any easier.

I wrote the following in October 1998. Grandpap had died on September 11 of that year. So I already hated that day before 2001. Every day between his death and the writing of this, I cried. And while the tears for him have diminished over the years, I can always say, for him, I cried the other day. Just as I do for my brother.

I CRIED THE OTHER DAY

I cried the other day,
Just wishin' you were here
I miss you more than words can say.

I'd give anything for more times to share
Like when you taught me to tie my shoe.
No matter what it was, you always seemed to care
Whether it was a little league baseball game
Or what I was to major in.
Though in old age, you were tame
You always had a story of what you've done and where
    you've been.

I cried the other day
Because I missed the laughs we had
You always had a joke to make me smile,
Though most of them were bad.
I remember staying at your house
And making cornbread in the wee morning hours.
You were always there to lend a helping hand
Whether it was a problem I had, or telling the cop I was in
    the shower.
You lived on this earth for ninety-five years
And you showed me to have no fears.

I cried the other day
And it was just for you
I just want to hold your hand for a little while
And see that twinkle in your eyes when you smile.
I again want to hear stories of yesteryear,
Like how you and your friends invented hockey.
But there will be no more stories of days gone by

Because the man who lived them stories is no longer here.
So every time I see a hummingbird fly,
It will bring a tear to my eye
And forever, I'll say,
For you, I cried the other day.

Even though his wasn't the first death I had suffered in my life, he was the first very close person I knew who died. I felt his death was unbearable, and we knew it was coming. When we don't know, it's so much more unbearable, especially when death arrives at our doorsteps in such an unspeakable manner.

CHAPTER 31

The Three Times Bub Was Sick

As I was growing up, my brother was enormous to me, even in his small stature. Though he was only five foot four and around 130 pounds, I surpassed him in height when I was probably thirteen or fourteen years old. It didn't matter. He was a giant to me, always and forever my little big brother. He seemed invincible, indestructible. I couldn't imagine anything ever happening to him that would make him appear weak, because he never was.

So, the time he came home from college on break looking like a skeleton scared me. He had no energy and wanted to sleep all the time. I had always heard people gained weight in college, but here was my hero of a brother losing weight. I remember clearly one day he was curled up, sleeping on the footstool of an old wooden chair. I tried to rouse him, but he wouldn't wake up. Our mom made him go to the doctor. His blood sugar was tested and found to be somewhere around 1000. The normal range is 70 to 110, so you can imagine how terrible he felt. It took a long time for him to recover, and he left Ohio Northern to take time off and get better. I know he always regretted that, because he loved being there. He could run track year-round there: cross country in the fall, indoor track in the winter, and outdoor track in the spring. He was in his element.

Not only that, but he also became a disc jockey for the college radio station. His DJ name was Jammin' Jerry. It always cracks me up when I hear that. Even to this day, I can't imagine my shy and reserved brother on the radio, talking and playing music. The idea makes me laugh.

Just after New Year's in 2001, my mom called me while I was hanging out at my friend Jackie's house. We were getting ready to go back to Mount Union, where we attended together. My mom said I needed to come home and take her to my brother's apartment. He needed to go to the emergency room. I told Jackie I needed to go, and she told me to go. She loved my brother too; they ran cross country together. It normally took about twenty minutes to get to our house from Jackie's. I made it that day in twelve.

When we started out for Pittsburgh, the temperature dropped, and a freezing rain began to pound us as we drove. I was driving my mom's car, still going 60 to 70 miles an hour on the highway. We slid, skidded, and swerved through the thickening slush and ice on the roads. To this day, I believe Grandpap Chase helped us on that journey. We needed the hand of an angel, that's for sure.

When we arrived at Bub's apartment, we thought he was dead. He was lying on the couch, not moving. The stench of sickness filled the air. He had the flu and was the sickest person I had ever seen. We loaded him into the car. I had to practically carry him and put him in the back seat. He was moaning in pain, clutching a bag in which he'd already thrown up twice in the short time we'd been there. My mom asked Bub where his roommate was, and he replied, "He has been out partying since the other day." He said he tried to call his roommate but he never responded. Apparently, this behavior was not uncommon for him.

We got him to the hospital, and his condition was dire. Because his blood sugar was over 1500, the medical team promptly placed him on an insulin drip. He was in ketoacidosis and extremely dehydrated. They hooked him up to a saline drip and medication for nausea and started an antibiotic drip because they believed the respiratory infection had led to pneumonia. He was in the hospital for four or five days on a constant insulin drip until his sugar returned to normal.

I returned to college before he was discharged, so my mom picked him up and took him home. His roommate was there that time, and according to Bub, the scene of our mom ripping him a new one for leaving her son alone when he was sick was scary to behold.

Another time he was sick, we were both still living with our parents. I was twelve, and he was sixteen. I had contracted the chickenpox on December 11, so I got to miss a week of school until Christmas vacation started. It was great for me; I got an extra-long vacation. I was cleared days before Christmas Day, so we thought it was safe for me to attend family festivities. Turns out it wasn't me we needed to worry about.

On Christmas night, after we returned home, Bub complained to our mom about not feeling great. She checked him over and saw the telltale signs of chickenpox. Dutifully, our mom made calls to the family to let them know he had them. One of our aunts started screaming at our mom about how she should have known better than to bring him around the family if she knew he was sick. We didn't know, of course. He showed no signs until we got home. I felt terrible. I had gotten to miss school, but Bub got the chickenpox on Christmas Day and didn't get to enjoy the benefits of being sick, only the shitty parts. He also had to miss a trip he had planned with his friends. He was so mad at me. I have to admit it was kind of funny to me because he had picked on me about the blotches on my face. I felt terrible about it, however.

These were the only times I really remember him ever being sick. He just seemed so indestructible.

CHAPTER 32

Eternal Burdens

J erry Eugene "Bub" Blackburn Jr. died February 22, 2008. He is survived by his mother, Rose; his father, Jerry; his brother, Robbie; and numerous cousins, aunts, uncles, and friends.

We learn to go on, somehow, some way. We find ways to do it. Sometimes we use means that are good and healthy; sometimes we fall into the darkness of our own demons. Moving on is inevitable, at least in the context of time passing. Moving our hearts, our souls, and our grief down that line is much more difficult, seemingly impossible. Sometimes we find ourselves circling back to the beginning, stuck in a pattern of despair. Not all the roads we travel are straight. There are many detours, closure signs, and BRIDGE OUT signs that stop us from a smooth way ahead. We do our best, though, looking into our mirrors to see the past as it was and feel the love that we shared. We look especially for the moments that we didn't know were going to be special until long after those times were gone. God or whatever entity doesn't provide instructions for these fragile, brief lives. So we just do the best we can while we have them.

I think one of the things that gets lost over time is the richness of memory. Like old photographs, in time they fade. God or genetics has blessed me and given me a decent memory; I can still recall things all these years later. I hope that by writing this, I am making Bub proud. I am using my writing—what he said is a tremendous talent I have—to honor him. To make him live long beyond 2008. Again, going back to the *Dark Tower* series, quoting a conversation between Roland and Eddie:

> "Is he a man?" Roland asked.
> "I think he is, and not just because of what John Cullum said.
> It's what I feel here." Eddie patted his chest above the heart.

"So do I."

"Do you say so, Roland?"

"Aye, I do. Is he immortal, do you think? Because I've seen much in my years, and heard rumors of much more, but never of a man or woman who lived forever."

"I don't think he needs to be immortal. I think all he needs to do is write the right story. Because some stories do live forever."

Understanding lit up Roland's eyes. At last, Eddie thought. At last, he sees it.

I am telling the story of my loss, my family's loss of a life that was much too brief, albeit well lived. We keep him alive in our hearts daily, in our minds constantly, and in our stories periodically. He deserved so much more life than what he was given. Many people do, but, to quote a lyric from another band he influenced me to love, Live, from their album *Mental Jewelry* (which he also purchased for me), "The pain is right here where I am." That it is, forever and always. "Always," as Severus Snape says about his love for Lily Evans in *Harry Potter*. The pain never really lessens with the passage of time. I think much like anything else, we can grow used to its burden. We won't know how heavy a burden it was until we put down, if we ever get to. Some burdens, though, are eternal, like a good story. They live on forever. Especially when you hold the kind of guilt I felt because I believed I killed my brother with a thought.

CHAPTER 33

Dreams Achieved

"What happens when I get to thirty-three?" I asked in a poem. Here we are at thirty-three. The journey of official chapters ends here. It has been a ride, that's for sure. Memory Lane is pitted with many obstacles, both sweet and bitter. We ingest them both, for memories are all we have, and we say we love them all. Our taste for the bitter ones has developed over the years to where our eyes don't water as often as they used to; on occasion, though, they still have the power to get us again. And they always will, no doubt. This will be the last turn on that lane as we head for home, to put our heads down and hope for rest, perchance to dream of things lost but not forgotten. In dreams, hugs can almost be felt; they are almost real. Almost. What is always real, though, is the love. The love. The love.

The last story I will tell is the one we as a family are the most proud of. I think I can speak for my mom and dad about that. It started as an acceptance letter from Ohio Northern University in 1994 and ended with a degree from Point Park College after nearly seven years. He was on the eight-year plan. We all have different paths. Some are straight lines. More often than not, they meander, with many switchbacks, detours, and downright closures along the way.

Bub started at Ohio Northern University, then took time off because of his health concerns, as I stated earlier. Then he enrolled at a technical college, ITT Tech in Pittsburgh. Hated it. He said, "I could teach the classes there because they don't have a clue."

After that, he tried the Pittsburgh Technical Institute. He was there for a short time and complained about similar things. They weren't teaching him what he needed to know.

He then started at Point Park College. It was more expensive than the other schools, which he hated, but they were going to give him the future he desired. This was the means to his most meaningful goal. That goal was set in motion when he was a young child as he played with his electrical sets for kids and took things apart to see how they went together. He would take radios apart and wire them back together again. He would add speakers and play the songs and bands that, many years later, are still my favorites—the "good sounds," as Momma Mott would say. When he got older, he developed his wiring prowess by setting up elaborate systems in his cars with amplifiers and multiple speakers. He wanted the music to penetrate the soul, not through the ears but through every pore of the skin. Music meant that much to him. He used his skills, ingrained knowledge, and talents to bring the music to him in a way that meant more than just being able to turn it up loud. He wanted to experience the music, not just listen to it.

He graduated from college after following a path that was as unique as him. He lived his dreams. He achieved his dreams. And now we hope to see him in ours.

Epilogue

So that's it, the story of how I loved and lost my brother. I do apologize for the things I got wrong, the ones I misrepresented, and the stories I left out. Apologies to anyone who wasn't asked to share a story and wishes they had been, and to anyone who feels shorted in these pages. The first one, though, about anything I got wrong, I do sincerely apologize for. I wanted to get everything right, but, to use another Rolandism from the *Dark Tower* series, the past is in drift. Our memories change over time, whether because we forget minute details, we change them to smooth them out, or some other factor. We change our memories over time. They are rarely ever one hundred percent accurate. That's why eyewitness testimony at trials is notoriously dicey. With that being said, I did the best I could. Besides, I wrote this for three reasons. The first was to bring my brother back to life in the only way I know how. The second was to try to make him proud. I hope I did that. The third reason was to try to slow down the spiral of my grief—for, as I've said before, that circle, or wound if you prefer, never closes.

Appendix: The Poems

THE SCHOOL YEAR HAS COME TO AN END
I HAVE NOTHING, BUT MAYBE A NEW FRIEND
BUT ONLY ONE OR TWO
HOW MANY MORE DAYS;
ONLY A FEW

LIFE WILL SOON BE A BORE AGAIN
A BASEBALL GAME HERE AND THERE
THAT WE JUST CAN'T WIN.

THE DAYS WILL GROW HOTTER
AS, THANKFULLY, MY LIFE GROWS SHORTER
DAYS OF LONELINESS WILL PLAGUE ME
LIKE A BAD COLD.

TWO MORE YEARS IN THIS HELL
THEN I'LL BE GONE
OUT OF THIS SHITHOLE
NEVER TO BE SEEN AGAIN

MY LIFE WILL BE OVER
NOTHING TO SHOW
EXCEPT A COUPLE OF SO-CALLED FRIENDS
WHO LEFT ME A LONG TIME AGO.

BROTHER

You're my brother,
My family,
My friend and foe
Everywhere you went,
I wanted to go.
I wanted to be just like you
No matter what you wanted to do,
I still can't believe what happened
Since then, it's been a life of confusion
Every day I wake up
Praying for a delusion.
Never before have I wished
To be insane
But I'd do anything
To get that fucking memory
Outta my brain
You're my brother
And I want to make you proud
I miss you more
Than should be allowed.
You're my big brother
And I'm the little
And together we make a pair
We are a tandem
And that
We'll always share
You're my little big brother
And will always be
But what happens
When I hit thirty-three?

WAKING NIGHTMARE

I've lost my thought

In truth, lost it all

I have nothing left

Just a few words

Take me down

I have no swords

Nothing in reserve

I have no defense

I shatter I crack

I haven't been the same since

I try to laugh

To keep from crying.

I fetch a deep breath

But end up only sighing

Someone once told me

To get over

It's done and gone

But what they

Don't know

is I

Can't let it go

It's there

Every night like a

Never ending picture show

Loop and repeat

Pounding a

Beat beat beat beat

In my head

Every night and day

A waking nightmare

A sleeping scream

No rest for the wicked
Or the weary
It's a constant battle
I lost my ground
No advantage gained
Just a life where nothing
Is quite the same
Just about
Everything changed
Except my name.
I still blame
God
And why not
I was told
He has the shoulder
To hold
This boulder
While I
Sit and smolder
My life fading
As I get older
I have anger
In bunches
Like welfare
Kids in line
Getting free lunches
Everything I see
I can't take
Because I put my fist
In it and fucking break
I don't care for pain
I can't feel it right now
Fuck this all
Let me out now

Strike me down

I don't care how

All bets are off

Anything is allowed

I've done enough

I've made some proud

Let me end it now

I can't fucking stand

To hear

One more wow

I want to hit and bite

And claw and scowl

And put my fist

Right through their

Fucking mouth

Tears of pain

And rage

It's all the same

I'm a beast

Locked in a cage

I'm no longer afraid

Come and take me away

Fuck you and you

And fuck what you say

Am I back to even

This house money?

My debts paid?

Can I walk away?

Peace in mind

Settled in what I could

And couldn't find

More questions

Than answers

Tiptapping away

"HEY DICK"

Like tiny dancers
No comet or Cupid
Blitzen or prancer
Bringing gifts of knowledge
Just another winter
Eating up
The fall foliage.
Beating my head
Against the wall
Hoping it's been
A dream of this all
Hoping against hope
I never answered that call
Never answered that bell
That marked the moment
That I fell
And came apart
At the seam
That moment when I ceased
Being me.

THE PLAGUE

When dreams become plague

That filter out the day

All the fears that you've come to know

Make their appearance

When the eyes go closed

The darkness has become

A master of pretend

Leads me down the path

Telling I can go home again

I wish to not go

Back to where I've been

A world where tranquility

Is a mortal sin

I searched for peace

In what you'd call

The underground

Red sea reflected to the sky

What is up, where is down

All the questions asked

Except the why?

Quelling yawn as I tarry

Fight back

Fatigue I bury

I've grown more than just weary

Rest against the wall

In a moment before I fall,

The inevitable comes upon us all

Regardless of how much we stall

Plague comes

Mindless of a scream

Caring not about what it's done

"HEY DICK"

Tearing the world apart at the seam
Allowing for nothing
Not even a dream.

OMNIBENEVOLENT
NO MORE

Around four years ago today
My life changed
In an unthinkable way,
God or whatever
Took my brother's precious life away
So many people say
It'll get better
But it hasn't yet
I haven't had a single ounce
Of anger disperse
Day's number 1-4-6-2
And it still hurts
Getting no better
But probably worse
I wanna go outside
And scream and curse
Beat my chest
And let my vocal cords burst
No amount of physical pain
Can compete
with the pain
Of every heartbeat.
A thousand memories
Flooding my brain
All vying for the main screen
Which is dominated
Not by memory, but a dream
Where I'm looking on
Unable to move
Unable to scream,
I wake without relief

Just more anger buried deep
I've heard time and again
That this is God testing me
So, if that's the case,
Then I failed miserably
My faith has weakened
Not been renewed
God is no longer
What I viewed
All good and powerful
That idea is skewed
I think you don't care
All that much
We've fucked up over and over
So, you've washed your hands of us
So, we are here
Wallowing in what's left behind
You don't care if when
We are in trouble we look to the sky.
I know this is blasphemous
But I don't care
I am full of anger
And I need to direct it somewhere
Life has been fucked up
That ain't fair
So much wrong
So little right
Only escape
Is to sleep at night
But I suffer dreams
Of the past
Everything straining
Threatening the clasp
Sometimes I feel
I'm cracking like glass.

A ROSE BLOOMS

A rose blooms
In a time
When frosty morn looms
When the sign
Is season's change
In spring the flower
Is time to grow
When hope springs eternal,
And the grass will soon
Need a mow
Even in summer
During hottest days
The flower is expected
To stay
But not the fall
That's the end of all
No red or blue or white or pink
A birthday present from above
So just when I think
The tears were over
A rose blooms
In October.

THE LAST OF MY NAME

Started out with

Such an inappropriate laugh

You'd think my mind had cracked

It fricked and fracked

Sanity so far from a path

It's gone and lost track

Ticked and tacked

As time ticked and tocked

Therapy was suggested

But I balked

Went and just sat

I could talk

Epic circles cast

Words and words

And more words

But never mentioning the past

Like Roland

I am the last

At least in name only

Once I'm dead and gone

That'll be it, it's all done

There'll be no stories to carry on

Just how the west was won

I may be shunned

Or be the anti-hero

None of these outcomes

Is what I fear though

Yet I can't find the words

Words or more words

To bring my fear lighting

I've tried hundreds of times

Writing thousands of lines
As tears flow,
In the dead of night.

THAT WHICH IS LEFT BEHIND

When I woke up this morning

I didn't plan on dying

I'm sorry my number was called

And that you are now crying

I hate that I'll never finish that book

I don't know if I can forgive myself

For the vacations I never took

I wish I would have taken more time to relax

Maybe it would mean I'd still be alive, perhaps

I wonder where it goes

All the time that we have wasted

Maybe boredom is just another name for those

Times life has us hastened

I regret the news you've been informed

It was never my intention

To have your life's normalcy torn

From my name's mention

To have so many touching eulogies performed

In my honor

Maybe I should have never gone there

But in the end, our decisions are made

The price is paid

The path is laid

And we go about on our way

But I have regrets

And they are plenty

I focused too much on money

I arrived late and left early

I didn't say things that needed to be said

I stayed clean when I should have gotten dirty

I played a victim

When sometimes I was just a fool
I got hot when I should have played it cool
It sucks I'll never get to finish that series
It hurts me to think to myself
That I will be easy to forget
I hate myself a little for leaving behind
So much debt
I'm sorry that I left my house a mess
Who will explain it to my cats
About my death?

QUESTIONS AND ANSWERS

What would we do if
We Were given an answer
To every question why
What if every tear we ever cried
For reasons that were never a surprise,
What if we had the reason
Behind every lie
How would it feel to know
Everything you ever tried
Would turn out right
What if all the answers
Were kept inside
But we are just too blind
Hiding behind the cliche
That I am fine
What if the truth is within our grasp
But no matter how hard you tried,
You just couldn't make it last
It slipped away too fast
Another ship getting under way
Sails at full mast
What if all we had was
Just a little class
Another day gone by
Where we asked
For the reasons why
Just another truth
Inside, yet one more lie
One more deep breath
Shortened to a sigh
One last lonely tear,

That won't turn into a cry
So many questions
That none can answer
Another sleepless night
At least let us shake hands, sir
All these things
I was never meant to know
It's time to just let em go
Nothing good can come
From this mental picture show
Only one more day
Of feeling pretty low
Just need to live life
With all its ebbs and flow,
All those questions why
They can go where ever
Unanswered questions go to die
It's about to be my time
All the world could be mine
All I have to do is try.

SONGS WE KNOW,
DEPTH WE WERE UNSURE

You got to fight for your right

Tonight tonight

Otherwise it'll be

Good riddance, the time of your life

And when I'm gone

Ill just say

Bye bye bye

There'll be no

Tears in heaven

As long as you

Don't stop believin

And you don't let

Cold November rain

Steal your

Minutes to memories

It'll be rain on the scarecrow

Washing away the pain,

That will leave you

Insane in the brain

Leave

You feeling

Estranged

There will be no more

Bittersweet me

Just a hope for

Time stand still

Where you can

Dream on

Hoping everything won't be

Gone

And eventually everything will

Carry on

But just maybe

In the end

It'll just be

The end of the world as we know it

And life will have flashed by

In a New York minute

We will have

No excuses

Except this life was too

Hard to handle

But maybe I can

Hold on

To the right stuff

When all my life

It was

Because the night

And if I fell

You saved my life tonight

When I was

Right next door to hell.

WASTELAND

The featureless face of the demon
No sounds, only noiseless screaming
Painful tears on my cheek
Blazing paths of acidic streak
The world, now just an embodiment of time
Drink up, your thirst craves the blood-filled wine
Hope is lost in the darkest chasm
All I hear is laughter of brethren's sarcasm
All of time, another man's wasteland

The world moves on only for those who understand
The rest of us left behind choking on ill-repute
Comic relief as a deaf mute
Each day grows harder to bear
The doubling of my mind makes me unaware
Two places, two memory sets
I'm caught in a world of someone else's regrets
Two worlds whirling into oblivion
Can't figure out which is a dream
And which I have been living in
I scream out for help
And I'm burned by the sun and touched by the light of the
        moon
All together in one
Here lost in another world
Alone at the way-station
My heartbeat, my age hastened
Old before my time
Drink up, your thirst craves the blood-filled wine.

YOUR HEAVEN OR MINE?

Until we meet again
In a happier time
In your heaven
Or in mine
I bid you farewell
But not goodbye
Goodbye is forever
And I know that some day
We will be together
With laughs and smiles
Until then
I'll wait all the whiles
I'll hold my friend
And hope not
To descend
Until then
When we can begin
All over again
Start fresh and new
Become closer
Than ever have been
So few
You and me
Me and you
Let them see
It will be in heaven
We will be
Even if you don't agree
It'll be a happier time
And we shall be free

"HEY DICK"

No more numbers
Or disease
No more blunders
Only reprieve
No more thunder
Before a rainbow
Only holding on
And never letting go
It can be your heaven
Or it can be mine
As long as it's an eternity
Of you and me
That is just fine.

BIRTHDAY HUG

Happy Birthday brother

It's another year

Another number

And you're gone

And we are left here

All the pain

Still lingering on

It's been awhile

But the pain

Just won't reconcile

An open wound

Just left to fester

The hurt is an emotion

We just can't sequester

Everlasting

And eternal

No prosthesis or casting

No stitching

Could secure

And leave a scar

There'll never be closure

But it's your day

And I hope it's okay

That this is my way

To say happy birthday

I know you're in

Heaven above

But dammit

I need you here

To give you your

Birthday hug.

SONGS FOR THE PAST

Turn up the radio

Let the classics play

Give me one more chance

To put the future

On tape delay

I know every word

From that other world

I might miss a cue

And fumble a verse

But I'll belt them out

Like a hanging curve

Give me one more song

Let me just stay in the past

Let this be where I belong

Let me pour my soul

Into every line

Let it wash over me

Transplanting my place and time

Turn up the sound

While we're cruising around,

Good friends and family

Bonding through the music

Because in the music

We can't be touched

When you keep it inside

You'll never be crushed

It's a beauty that you can never hide

Turn up the radio

When it's playing

Something good

Let the classics flow

Let the memories flood
Just like they should.

HERO

36 hours
And a cloud of dust
Here comes the baby
And he don't weigh that much
In order to survive
He's going to need more than love
He needs someone that will match his blood
Two and a half months premature
Whether he'd survive
No one was really sure.
Then here comes the hero of this story
Still weary from delivery
She gave her blood
To her son, whom she already loved.
Fast forward now
To a later time
She in the stands
He on the field
Her, his number one fan,
Hardly ever missed a game
No matter the sports name
Always there
With the loudest cheer,
Then one day
In a flash
Everything was no longer ok
He, lying there in a pool of blood
She, knowing what needed to be done,
Tear drops his eye
Looking up, he thinks,
"Mommy, am I going to die?"

On now, to a later time

He, off to college

His time to shine

Her, at home

Her baby gone.

Thinks he is

Such a big man

Doesn't really understand

How truly cruel the world can be

On the phone every night

He thinks he is talking to

The love of his life.

But suddenly light

Turns too dark.

Mommy, your little boy

Has a broken heart.

This thought just won't leave

He just can't live

With broken heart disease.

He is going insane

He feels so ashamed

He feels he's lost the game

He takes the blame

For the shame

That came

With not using his brain.

Together, they got through

Two best friends

Doing for each other

Whatever they could do.

Now things are better

She says, "I love you"

He says, "whatever"

But if you will notice

"HEY DICK"

Both phrases have eight letters
He's just a little quirky
Some might even say dorky
For the things he thinks of,
But this is his way of expressing love.
Everyone has heroes
And when they come around, fear goes away
Some use athletes, actors or the like
And that's ok,
But he, he don't need any of them
He spells hero a different way
M-O-M.

UGLY TRUTH

I ain't dead
But I'm dying
I ain't sad
But I'm crying
I ain't worth much
But I'm trying
I ain't there
And you ain't here
But right now, it doesn't matter
Because I don't want to be
Anywhere.
I'm alive
But I'm not living
I'm tired and beaten
But I'm not giving
I'm alone
But I'm not scared
I have a phone
But it's not ringing
I feel nothing
So I guess this is apathy
I just live day by day
You can get me to smile
But not get me happy
I wish I could remember
And live the rest of my life
In last December
Back when I thought I knew
What pain really was
Now I don't have to think
It's everlasting in my heart

"HEY DICK"

There are no words
Just the silence
And I know
Because I am listening
And I just hope it's something
That I'm missing
This is pain at its widest breadth
I have people but I feel so alone
And I wish for death
With every breath.
But I still just get up every day
And live and being fake
In every way
And I block the truth at every turn
Because this is one truth
I never wanted to learn.

THE HIDDEN CRIMES OF MAN

I can no longer live with this deceit
It's time that I must admit defeat
I am here to lay my sword at your feet
I tried to be strong, but it turns out I'm weak
I tried for more but just couldn't keep

I looked for purpose in between the lines
I stared so long I missed all the signs
Persecute me for I committed so many crimes
I forgot what I couldn't remember so many times
I forged lies with so many "I'm fines"

I couldn't see but for the trees
I fell down upon the streets
Scraped and scabbed up my knees,
I wondered about the purpose of this disease
How many times can we live as we bleed?

I wondered about life without you
I questioned what I would do
I wanted the pain that's true
I wanted to feel my life gone askew
I just didn't care how, what, or with who.

I accept all the blame
Leave it at my doorstep in my name
It's my fault I'll never be the same
My fault there's only a flicker to where there used to be
    flame
I am forever consumed by my shame

"HEY DICK"

I accept if you hate me
It's the way things should be
I just had to see
I would hate me
I do hate me for how I wanted things to be

I wish I could take it back
My repugnant selfish act
I can't and that's a fact
I long for all the things I lack
I am consumed for having no tact
I will never forgive myself for that.

I CRIED THE OTHER DAY

I cried the other day,
Just wishin' you were here
I miss you more than words can say.
I'd give anything for more times to share
Like when you taught me to tie my shoe.
No matter what it was, you always seemed to care
Whether it was a little league baseball game
Or what I was to major in.
Though in old age, you were tame
You always had a story of what you've done and where
you've been.

I cried the other day
Because I missed the laughs, we had
You always had a joke to make me smile,
Though most of them were bad.
I remember staying at your house
And making cornbread in the wee morning hours.
You were always there to lend a helping hand
Whether it was a problem I had, or telling the cop I was in
the shower.
You lived on this earth for ninety-five years
And you showed me to have no fears.

I cried the other day
And it was just for you
I just want to hold your hand for a little while
And see that twinkle in your eyes when you smile.
I again want to hear stories of yesteryear,
Like how you and your friends invented hockey.
But there will be no more stories of days gone by

"HEY DICK"

Because the man who lived them stories is no longer here.
So every time I see a hummingbird fly,
It will bring a tear to my eye
And forever, I'll say,
For you, I cried the other day.

About the Author

Robbie Blackburn is a poet and storyteller whose work delves into the raw depths of human emotion. A seasoned caregiver with 23 years of experience in healthcare, Robbie brings compassion and authenticity to his writing, exploring themes of love, loss, and resilience. In his memoir, *Hey Dick: How I Loved and Lost My Brother*, he offers an intimate reflection on grief and the enduring bond of family. Also the author of *The Darkness Within*, Robbie explores the darker sides of human nature. He lives in Ohio with his wife and their cherished cats, finding inspiration in history, thought experiments, and life's quiet moments.

www.ingramcontent.com/pod-product-compliance
Lightning Source LLC
Chambersburg PA
CBHW071725120626
46550CB00002B/391